# FLASH
# FORWARD:
## A GUIDE TO SHAPING YOUR FUTURE

## LILY-THERESE WILTFONG

FOREWORD BY DOROTHY MacNEVIN, Ph.D.

# FLASH
# FORWARD:
## A GUIDE TO SHAPING YOUR FUTURE

ISBN-13: 978-0-9913513-0-5

Printed in the U.S.A.

Library of Congress Cataloging-in-Publication Data is available.

www.LilyTherese.com

# BOOK DEDICATION AND ACKNOWLEDGEMENTS

THIS BOOK IS DEDICATED to my husband, Vernon O. Wiltfong, who inspired, encouraged, and supported me throughout the writing of this manuscript. Vern, you are the everlasting love of my life, my strength, my spirit, and my voice when I am wordless. Thank you! This book is also warmly dedicated to my children: Raymie, Jennifer-Robyn, and Michael. Thanks also to my greatly treasured siblings, and all other significant family members. All of you are special threads of life woven deeply into my heart and the fabric of my being. Thank you!

A special thanks to my loving grandson, Michael Daniel, for your inspiration and faith. A special thanks to my talented sister, Liz-Ann Konn, and my husband, Vern Wiltfong, for the beautiful art illustrations for this book. Liz Diaz, I appreciate your continuous assistance, encouragement and warm friendship. Thank you for being my go-to person for the past several years. Thank you, Professor Dorothy MacNevin, my professional colleague, long-time friend, and kindred spirit. I could not have completed this manuscript without your great advice, excellent editing suggestions, and beautiful foreword.

To my kind friends and loyal clients (you know who you are), thank you for making this book possible. Wendy Byle of Byle Design and Associates, Woodland Hills, California, thank you for your elegant book design and attention to detail. Special thanks to Susan Rice Alexander for your encouragement and strong intuitive sense. This manuscript is an act of devotion to all of our ancestors, whose perseverance and quest for meaning in life connects us eternally to their spirit. Finally, *Flash Forward* is dedicated to the memory of my loving parents and two brothers. They are all gone from this earth but they will never be forgotten because they live forever in my heart.

*Autumn 2013*

# FOREWORD

THERE ARE NO GREATER RESOURCES on this earth than the human mind, the human heart, and the human spirit. Yet they remain the greatest mysteries on earth. The "human condition" in which we find ourselves comes with an intellect that we see as superior to that of other living forms on earth. Yet there is much we do not know about the power of the human brain. We do know that each individual human brain is made up of over one hundred billion nerve cells. Despite the amazing discoveries in the field of neuroscience, we are far from understanding the intricate complexity of how the human brain actually operates. Nor do we fully understand how to tap into the potential power of our own brain! We know that the brain is the "processing and control center" for all of our actions, thoughts, and emotions. Yet we don't even have the language to account for the complicated layers of our "human condition" so we refer to the "mind" when we speak of cognitive or intellectual functions. We speak of the "heart" to refer to the anguish and ecstasy of emotional experience that is inherent in the "human condition." We speak of the "spirit" to refer to the intangible, inexplicable insights that profoundly influence our daily life.

These complex dimensions of our "human condition" serve to inform the totality of our living presence in the world. Yet we often feel helpless in the face of the burdens and sorrows that life bestows upon all of us. We can't help ourselves from asking questions and questioning answers in the face of the agonizing riddles of life. We seek a reliable way to navigate the troubled waters of unknown dangers that threaten to engulf us in a dark sea of anonymity. We do not want to be tossed about in an ocean of victims adrift without purpose or meaning or mercy. Often feeling we have no control over our fate, we seek ways to stay afloat in our perilous predicament. We pursue knowledge through education. We have more knowledge and the planet has more educated people than ever before in the history of humankind. Yet that knowledge is not enough to guide us or our children or their children into an unknown future. Knowledge has never been enough to sustain human beings as they seek to minister to their intellectual, emotional, and spiritual needs. Through the ages, we have sought, not only food but fulfillment.

Thus human beings have sought salvation through religion, recognizing that we cannot thrive without nourishment that goes beyond meeting our physical needs. To put it in biblical terms, "Man does not live by bread alone." A verse from the Koran captures the same truth: "If I had but two loaves of bread, I would sell one and buy some hyacinth for they would feed my soul." Yet many in the modern world feel undernourished by what organized religion has to offer. Today there are more churches, mosques, temples, and denominational brands than the world has ever seen. But the faithful of many faiths feel marginalized by dogmatism that denounces science or political fanaticism that brutalizes human values.

Surrounded by the alluring sights and sounds of modern technology, we are besieged on all sides by slick "self-help" or "pop psychology" slogans that promise a plethora of "quick-fix" recipes to Hollywood-style happiness. But eventually this kind of junk food tends to starve rather than sustain the human spirit. So it is not surprising that many of us, although well-fed, well-clothed, affluent and educated, feel homeless and hungry, vulnerable and lost in the urban, global jungle. We cannot deny our insatiable craving for self-understanding and the depth of our appetite for authenticity in connecting with others. We are hungry for love. We are hungry for wisdom. We have a need to dream. Dreaming is not a frivolous dessert that is an optional item on the human. Dreaming is not ornamental; it is a fundamental feature of what makes us human. We need to dream, to expand our capacity for dreaming, and to be inspired and empowered to make our dreams come true. We long for our hearts to sing!

Lily-Therese understands all this. But she does not lecture. Nor does she preach. She sings to us from the pain and joy of her own personal journey toward self-discovery. She offers something as rare and sparkling as pure-cut diamonds—common-sense wisdom expressed in common-sense terms that you can carry with you for the rest of your life. Savor this book. Allow her song to capture your heart and launch you on your own steep journey to discover your higher self. The view from the top of the mountain is worth the climb and will cause your heart to sing.

*Dorothy MacNevin, PhD, California Polytechnic University, Pomona*

# A SPECIAL MESSAGE FROM LILY-THERESE

*F*LASH *FORWARD: A GUIDE TO SHAPING YOUR FUTURE* is the result of over forty-five years of professional experience as an Intuitive Specialist and Holistic Life Coach. Although I have studied metaphysics, holistic healing, and human spirituality in depth, no prestigious university degree hangs in my office. My knowledge and understanding of dreams is not acquired from the study of dream interpretation, but rather from my strong intuitive sense regarding the simple premonitory dream as a forewarning of a future event or experience. Intuition, common sense, observation, and the hard knocks of life have been my greatest teachers.

Direct experiences with people and nature have been very valuable sources of information and knowledge. I have learned much from my outside physical world, but I could not have written this book without the inner guidance from the Universal Spirit that unites us all. If you put aside your doubts and concerns you too will benefit from inner wisdom as it is revealed in your dreams, intuition, nature, symbols, and observation.

I am now in the winter season of my life, and this book offers both an ending and a new beginning for me. I was born clairvoyant. At a young age, I discovered that I could often see beyond the physical boundaries of time and space. In the physical world, there are some experiences that defy explanation and imply there is more to life than what the physical senses reveal. An inquisitive mind definitely gave me the incentive to seek answers to some of these puzzling incidents. When describing these occurrences I will provide my own interpretations as I have come to understand them. *Flash Forward* gives plenty of simple, real-life examples of future knowing that includes some of my personal experiences.

I have always had a strong desire to know how the human mind can sometimes predict future events. Over time, I learned that our beliefs, superstitions, and choices control and determine much of our future through habit. The subconscious plays a major role in helping to shape the future. Past programming can blindside you into believing that your destiny is controlled by predetermined fate or random chance. It may be that what we think of as random chance is really only the outcome of a chain of events in which the original cause is not recognized or is simply forgotten. I believe that any thought or choice that is repeated can become a habitual pattern that will continue to reproduce itself in your physical world as an outcome that contributes to shaping your future.

It is important to understand that your past, your present, and your future are intimately linked. Even though the future is not here yet, it still exists in the present time as potential. If you know what is happening in the present time, you can predict the probable outcome of many of your choices. Paying attention to your daily experiences can reveal what will be happening soon. As a result, *coming times can be perceived today when the human mind extends its capacity to see future probabilities.*

Looking ahead allows you to rethink your current experiences from another perspective. A sudden flash of insight can unlock another level of understanding. As the mind opens to new possibilities, your intuition, dreams, and gut-level feelings become valuable sources of guidance. Increased awareness of inanimate objects and omens from nature can also provide reliable information about the future.

To benefit the most from this manuscript, use your physical senses to connect you to the words you are reading. Then use your intuition to take you beyond the words to a new sense of inner-knowing. *Flash Forward* will introduce you to endless possibilities to provide you with a treasure of opportunities to shift your perception from the unknown to the known in a heartbeat. This book offers some practical ways of knowing the future as well as some unconventional methods that cannot always be logically explained. However, they work.

Finally, I have written this book in response to the growing number of questions posed by my clients and friends regarding the future, and how to solve perplexing human problems. Although it is based on thousands of case histories, I respect the privacy of my clients, and personal intuitive sessions always remain private and confidential.

I want to thank you for reading my book. Remember, you live in a physical world, but you are much more than your physical body and emotions. You are composed of body, mind, and spirit. Your magnificent potential lies within you just waiting to unfold. You are a powerful human being, and, as with the majestic eagle, it is your destiny to fly high above the storms and trials of life. Therefore, my friends, spread your cosmic wings and soar with me throughout the pages of this book. I shall be your guide, pointing to the signposts that reveal coming times to help you avoid the pitfalls of life.

As you encounter life challenges after reading this book, simply quiet your mind and listen. Intuitively, you will hear my silent words of encouragement because time and space cannot separate us spiritually. I hope that this book makes a difference in the quality of your life. You have made this book possible, and it is my legacy to you. May your journey around the Wheel of Life be blessed, and may you pass safely through the gateway of change, empowered by a new understanding of the potential you possess to shape your own future.

## About This Book

This manuscript is a guide to shaping your future. It is divided into three parts. The first portion is devoted to a wide range of messages about the future and the many sources through which these messages come. Real life examples reveal how your future is controlled by your subconscious, core beliefs, fears, memories, and sometimes the superstitions that make up your personal outlook on life.

The second portion is devoted to dreams in general, but it features the simple right-in-your-face-forewarning, known as the premonitory dream, because this is the one that grabs your attention. A premonitory dream can help you see into the future before it happens and serve as a forewarning that can be taken as face value, just as it appears. It can also be symbolically linked to a state of mind that is influenced by recent thoughts and feelings about your real life issues. To get its inner meaning, your personal under-standing of the symbols that appear in your premonitory dreams must be linked to your current life challenges which have triggered the forewarning.

The third portion is devoted to information about powerful tools that you can learn to use to help you prepare for change and future challenges. It introduces you to information that could keep you from being blind-sided, stuck and afraid to move forward on the Wheel of Life. Here you will find the fundamental ideas and concepts that reveal the foundational wisdom upon which the book is based. Finally, you will receive guidance on how to develop your own Flash Forward Plan to help you get started in shaping your future.

*Many Blessings,*
*Lily-Therese Wiltfong*
*Autumn 2013*

# TABLE OF CONTENTS

# CHAPTER ONE

# Can We Foresee the Future?

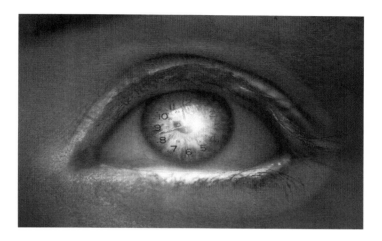

THE WORLD IS CONSTANTLY CHANGING, and that makes it appear to be unpredictable if you are not paying attention to your present moment. To the unaware individual, the future appears to be hidden, mysterious, and completely controlled by outside forces or fate. However, in most cases, the future is not beyond the scope of the logical mind's ability to think and plan ahead. The rational mind can anticipate coming times, but intuition takes you right into the future and returns with a sudden flash of information that was not previously known or available. Intuition is a mental process of the mind that is not fixed in time or predetermined by fate. Intuition shuts up reason and operates beyond the gut-level emotional knowing of instinct. The words *intuition* and *instinct* are used interchangeably, but, basically, the difference is that intuition is a direct guide to some mental powers of the mind and instinct is a direct guide to some capacities or functions of the physical body.

Instinct uses your feelings, the language of the subconscious, to speak to you. Your emotions developed long before the thinking part of your conscious brain, and today these still influence your actions and choices out of habit. Your feelings are mostly your fixed physical reactions to your environment. Goose bumps, tingling, sweating, and anxiety communicate your automatic response to the world around you. Sometimes your strong emotions bypass common sense because you lose control of your feelings to fear. As a result you are conditioned by the past automatically to repeat unintentional responses that limit new choices. This can be frustrating and lead to mistakes or other situations that repeat themselves like old vinyl records stuck in a groove. Despite past programming, time and experience have taught us that the mind can work with the feelings to initiate change and make better decisions to anticipate the future.

Your gut-level feelings or instincts also guide and warn you about the future. Sometimes you can pick up on things subconsciously through your feelings. Of course, you can also miss some red flags completely. For example, a gut-level feeling can be felt as queasiness, intestinal cramps, or a sinking discomfort in your stomach before you get fired from your employment. You may have sensed that your job was in jeopardy days ago, but your conscious mind may have ignored it or just not recognized the earlier premonition. Nevertheless, your gut feelings needed no facts, evidence, or explanation to get the message and give it back to you physically as a warning. If you had acted on your earlier hunch, you could now be working for another company.

Many of you experience knowing some of the future through your feelings. A sudden urge to take some form of action can help you anticipate something before it happens. If you can anticipate and identify certain tendencies already developing, other choices can be made to alter a future outcome. Intuition may not have all of the bells and whistles of your gut-level feelings, but it can combine instinct with common sense to help you make crucial decisions to keep you alive. Strong hunches have saved my life on several occasions. If I had stopped to think before acting on a powerful gut-level feeling, I could now be dead.

**Recognize Authentic Gut-Level Feelings**
You can fail to recognize your authentic gut-level feelings when your fear-based emotions are out of control. Fearful emotions can limit decision making and lead you to repeat the same old choices out of habit. When your strong emotions affect your state of mind, you better think twice before trusting your instinct. Sometimes it is necessary to test your hunches before acting on them. You must be able to tell the difference between an authentic gut-level feeling and an emotional snap judgment

that is based on prior conditioning. There is a definite relationship between the two, but there is also a distinct difference that you must understand.

An instinctive response is a physical reaction to a situation or external threat to the body. Fear is a primitive instinct that is hot wired into your subconscious to help you stay alive. When adrenalin kicks in as fight-or-flight it does not require thinking because it is an automatic response. In comparison, an emotional snap judgment is the physical body's response to a fearful thought that is interpreted by the mind but is not physically life threatening. Fearful thoughts can cause past programming to affect your current decisions that have nothing to do with physical survival. Out-of-control fears can significantly affect your perception of reality and interfere with your genuine gut-level feelings when the mind imagines itself to be in a life-or-death situation.

Your conscious mind can overreact to situations based on past experiences and interfere with your gut feelings by giving the mind the wrong signals. Strong emotions related to an incident that happened years ago can trigger a predisposition to respond in a similar way that has nothing to do with your authentic gut-level feelings or the present time. For example, a new woman at your workplace may provoke a disturbing snap judgment from you without a logical reason. An instant dislike without a word exchanged needs to be questioned because the source may not be an authentic gut feeling. Your feelings could be triggered by your fears, anger, and jealousy simply because the woman resembles the one that stole your job or your ex-husband a long time ago. Think before you respond, and sort through your feelings before reacting on your emotions alone. Your gut feelings in this case should not be trusted because they are based on emotional memories and past experiences that are not life-threatening today.

## Repeated Choices Create Repeated Experiences

You can develop psychological blind spots when you do not look at your problems from several different perspectives. Programmed, habitual thinking can keep you chained to the same repeated choices in the dead zone of immobilization. If you are too rigid in your thinking, old thought patterns will repeat themselves based on your past choices, feelings, and expectations, which will make you predictable. When past issues and problems that we thought we buried years ago rise up again like zombies to haunt us, we eventually seek solutions and answers.

Constant social problems and challenges force us to change the way we look at our experiences. They move us out of our comfort zone and reveal all of our issues. We may blame fate or other people for our circumstances, but when we finally stop resisting change, we find that some forced changes are really blessings in disguise. Negative life experiences may really be "good news" because they can force us to expand our view to see the bigger picture. This takes us out of the twilight zone of procrastination, and we begin to move with the flow of change instead of fighting it.

## Do Not Procrastinate

Some things can keep you blocked from seeing the truth about your life situations. Self-deception and procrastination are the biggest robbers of your choices and ability to see the future. A little peek into the future can indicate coming times, but if you wait too long to recognize a problem it may be too late to change an outcome. The time to make most changes is before they are forced upon you. Sometimes, uncertainty and fear of change can interfere with your control over future outcomes, but you can reconsider your situation and make other decisions while you still have options. When you are stuck at a crossroad, consider your current circumstances and other possible courses of action you can take today to modify your situation.

You can learn to recognize patterns that reveal present tendencies or clues to the future. What are you experiencing right now in a particular area of your life that is hinting at a future outcome? Your subconscious is programmed to help you survive, if you don't freeze in fear or denial. If your conscious mind takes no action and does nothing to protect itself from obvious warnings, you will experience the consequences. If you have been noticing red flags and still don't get the warning, now is the time to start asking yourself, "What is most likely to happen if I take no action or if I make other choices?"

I ask you in return, what is your common sense telling you to do? Your common sense can anticipate future probabilities. What are your gut-level feelings telling you to do? Apprehension, strong hunches, and other obvious signals from your "sixth sense" could be shouting at you to do something *now*. Intuition is not limited to just the thinking and feeling parts of you. Intuition is more subtle, but it can take you instantly to another level of knowing.

## Tools that Enhance Perception

It is important to understand that your past, your present and your future are intimately linked. Common sense is a fundamental ability to perceive your daily life experiences and link them to your future. You may not usually think of common sense as a necessary quality in shaping your future. However, failing to make this connection can seriously limit your ability to perceive reality, initiate change, and make other choices. Remember, your perception of life is the way you see things formed by your core beliefs, fears, memories, and sometimes the superstitions that make up your personality.

Your beliefs filter all of your physical senses, affecting your perception in every area of your life. To enhance your understanding of reality, you may have to change how your perceive it. Life is a lot easier when you can see the bigger picture by connecting your life experiences to some of your choices instead of blaming outside forces, such as predetermined fate or random chance. It may be that what we call random chance is really only the outcome of a chain of events in which the original cause is not recognized. If you look from only one narrow point of view, your conscious mind may block out intuition, omens, symbols, impressions, visions, and dreams.

Sometimes your perception of the future is improved when you can look ahead, but in order to zero in on the future you must also look behind at what you already know about a particular situation. Looking at your daily experiences can help you see around corners to change outcomes before the future happens. When you begin to observe a certain pattern in your thinking, you will be able to predict tomorrow if things continue moving in the same direction as today. You can link your choices with your experiences in a cause-and-effect relationship, so that forethought, anticipation, and precaution can detect probabilities along a current course. Thinking things through can help you make informed decisions and prevent potential mishaps before they occur. When the conscious mind knows all it can about a matter, intuition steps in to fill in the unknown.

To anticipate coming times, you must be able to adapt to changing circumstances. You can improve self-observation, life experiences, choices, and habits. Inner-change does not come about magically or overnight. The processes of self-observation and self-questioning provide you with perspectives for self-understanding and self-directed change. Awareness training is another powerful tool for staying in touch with the here and now because it helps you focus on what you are thinking, what you are doing, and how you are feeling. Listening and paying attention are other significant tools that prepare and alert you to changes in your environment and in your own physical body. These allow you to intervene to change a probable outcome by making other choices before the future occurs. When the curtains of the past are drawn open, you can easily observe certain patterns of thinking that will only change if you make a choice to do so.

## Change is Not the Enemy

You cannot afford to leave your future to chance or fate. You consciously influence the future when you set goals, pay attention to current conditions, and are willing to adapt to changes. The destiny that you want to experience involves conscious decisions and present-day actions toward your objectives. To embrace change, you must see it coming. To capture the power of external change, you must be willing to initiate the action of self-directed change.

Self-directed change gives you the foresight to look into tomorrow today to see your world from another perspective. It's easy to lose control to overwhelming surprises. Do you ever try to anticipate future events? What if you could flash forward into your future? Would you do it? A trial run through your future would reveal what you can expect in coming times. Do you ever ask yourself, "Why me?" when things go wrong? The instigator behind this experience in many cases is forced change. We all must deal with forced changes at some point. If you try to avoid your life lessons, the winds of change will bend you to the ground, pull you up by your roots, and give you a good shaking to awaken you.

## What About the Future?

The desire to see beyond today forces us to ask questions about the future. Can we really foresee the future? Are some things destined to happen? Is our fate written in the stars? Can dreams reveal coming times? What about you, my friend? Are you curious about your future? Can you predict where you will be one year from now? Have you ever longed for a way to overcome your own "psychological blind spots" to see what awaits you in the future? How clear is your vision of tomorrow? Are you looking, but not seeing? Are you listening, but not hearing? What are the hard knocks of life trying to tell you?

This book offers a broad range of answers to these intriguing questions. All of the real-life examples presented here can help expand your perception of your experiences and increase your ability to shape your own future.

## Learn to Read Everything

The unexpected can be seen in the present moment when you look beyond the physical. When you understand the relationship between all things, the holistic viewpoint expands your inner-knowing to reveal what is hidden to the conscious mind. This enhanced perception takes into account the body, mind, emotions, and spirit as one undivided whole. Even the environment is considered a part of the whole person.

A sense of interconnection to your surroundings can offer you important sources of guidance. Even inanimate objects can help you tap into omens and signs when you change the way you look at them. You must learn to see objects with more than just your physical eyes. Don't let inanimate physical forms fool you into believing that everything is not an integral part of you. When you expand your vision, your world reveals unlimited possibilities and potential sources of knowledge you never considered or were unable previously to see or access.

A sudden flash of insight, a dream, a message from nature, and even a warning from what looks like a lifeless object can offer you new information. When your inner door of perception opens, human progress steps in, initiating movement, change, and future seeing. Self-directed change will help you move beyond boundaries, old programming and procrastination. Simply making other choices can change your future. Get in touch with your sixth sense before making important decisions or choices. Your mind and feelings can work together to produce profound results.

Many people find it difficult to understand the connection between the body and mind, so they dismiss this reality as "New Age hocus-pocus." However, medical breakthroughs have affirmed many times that there is a definite connection between the mental realm of the mind and the physical realm of the body.

Modern technology can team up with ancient wisdom for a balanced approach to anticipate the future. Our ancestors had an instinctive understanding of the significance of omens from nature. From ancient times, people looked to symbols to deliver a message or indicate changing times. The behavior of wild animals, patterns of a flight of birds in the air, or a beautiful rainbow were significant messages to our early ancestors who were closely connected to their environment. Nature offered important meaning to their day-to-day lives.

Even in modern times, observing your environment can be powerful sources of insight, protection, instruction, and guidance. Pay attention to your hunches, omens and feelings on a daily basis. Your intuitive self will provide you with guidance and warnings of things yet to come. Remember, omens may materialize in many different forms that require your personal interpretations according to your present conditions or circumstances. The following pages will look at real life examples to demonstrate how the mind, feelings, and intuition work together to shape your future.

## CHAPTER ONE NOTES

## CHAPTER TWO
# Messages About Your Future

THE UNIVERSE IS CONSTANTLY FLASHING you the latest messages about you and your future. Once your mind accepts your interconnection to everything on Mother Earth, your environment offers an instant feedback of unlimited resources. You must understand that your subconscious is connected to everything in the universe. Even a falling star grabs your attention because it is a part of you. To expand your perception and intuition, you must see the connection between your mind, body, emotions, and environment. When you do, messages from different sources begin to reveal themselves to you in many forms.

Once you recognize your inner link to everything in your surroundings, you realize that nothing happens to you by chance or out of the blue. Mistakes, accidents, coincidences, nature, and even your wildest dreams have something to tell you. Sometimes you must look beyond your physical senses to get it. At other times all that you have to do is open your eyes to observe messages everywhere.

Where are you mentally and emotionally when something unusual occurs? What do your mind and gut-level feelings tell you? How can you associate nature with your current experiences? Can you connect a bird pooping on your car this morning with your boyfriend's dumping you last night? Are you constantly being dumped on by family members, friends, co-workers, and even strangers? Are you seeing a regular pattern of experiences that will repeat themselves in the future if you don't set some boundaries? What can you do to change an outcome? If you don't make new choices, be ready to run for cover when you see a flock of pigeons heading your way!

Don't ignore outcomes of chance, coincidences, or so-called mistakes because they appear to be unimportant or accidental. As Freud said, there are no accidents. Even a stranger in a public place can give you a warning message of coming times if you listen and act on what you are hearing. Indirect messages may apply to you. If you dismiss some signs as insignificant, you might miss that they are very important clues to your future. The more dramatic signs catch your eye, but everything has something to tell you whether it whispers or shouts.

Warning messages are external, physical clues that nature sends you as preventive measures. Sometimes if you miss a small red flag warning, nature has to resort to a more right-in-your-face dramatic signal before you get it! Watch for early warning signs that may appear to be coincidental or unimportant. There is a tendency to dismiss the significance of some meaningful messages. It is human nature to ignore advance warnings until it is too late to change an outcome. Use common sense and pay attention to little clues that will get worse if you continue to ignore them.

It is easy to miss little red flags completely when you don't connect them to your daily experiences. The following warning signals are some small premonitory messages that can lead to serious consequences if you miss them. Do not ignore a fender-bender, job termination, a dog biting you, your back going out, something dropping on your head, or even an accidental "butt-dialing." If you miss the initial little red flags, the more serious consequences could be a major accident, bankruptcy, house foreclosure, divorce, severe illness, painful injury, or even a drive-by shooting (especially if the gun is aimed at your head). Yes, these significant hard knocks of life could be the consequences of ignoring the initial little warnings, but now they have your full attention.

You must understand that information comes to you in many forms and from unusual sources. Your mind must also make the connection to your gut feelings to get the message. A broken-down car may reflect a breakdown in your own thinking or communication. A horn that does not work may reflect an inability to express yourself or indicate the need to communicate your feelings more often. Problems with your phone may reveal too much talking, so the message may be to put a lid on it. It may also be a sign to be silent or withdraw from activity. Some physical signs are messages of things that you must mentally release. A nervous breakdown is a loss of control, so the message is to learn to let go of your mental burdens each day instead of waiting for the bottom to fall out from under you. Taking on other people's burdens or problems can make you feel like you have a monkey on your back or several mischievous freeloaders. Learning to let go of mental and emotional burdens that are not your own can prevent a loss of control in your future.

Whatever happens in your outer world is always first reflected in your inner world of thought. Paying attention to the information that your physical senses give you regarding daily experiences will increase your ability to be aware of what your sixth sense is communicating to you. Warning messages can give you important information that may not be evident to the conscious mind. The world around you is full of signs, omens, symbols, and messages that await your discovery as you seek to unravel the mysteries of life. You do not need to climb the highest mountains of Tibet in search of a world-famous guru for answers. You need only remember that the day-to-day wisdom of nature is within your grasp, reminding you that shelter from the storm awaits you if you pay attention to your environment.

Your dreams and signs from the physical world hold significant information (dreams will be discussed in a later chapter). Your outer and inner world bring messages of your future to help you in the present time or to prepare you for avoiding disasters in the future. Continued failure, bad luck, heartache, and negativity are signposts that you need to make inner changes. Do not try to find solutions on the outside alone. Look deeply beneath your experiences. Question your point of view from every angle. Be honest with yourself. Your daily life is full of messages that you may not recognize or do not understand. There are messages everywhere, but they do you no good unless you can recognize them for what they are. The following are examples of messages that forewarned coming times.

## Jill Gets the Warning

Occasionally, messages to protect you can come through other people. Hearing people speak of their concerns and problems may also be indirect warnings. The messages that you receive when listening to other people chatting can provide you with information and a solution to your own troubles.

After a long day at work, Jill decided to pick up a medical prescription at the pharmacy. While waiting in line, Jill overheard a conversation between two men standing behind her about the danger of driving with bad car brakes. Another man soon joined in the lively discussion. Listening to the people talk reminded Jill of a problem she was having with her own car brakes. She had been procrastinating repairing the brakes on her car for the past five days.

Bingo! Jill got the message and the warning. Bad car brakes are an accident waiting to happen. As soon as she returned home, she called a brake repair shop to remedy the situation. Listening to the conversation in the pharmacy had served as a definite warning to Jill.

Likewise, paying attention to the fears and safety concerns of other people can definitely provide you with solutions to the dangers lurking in your own car and home or serve to help someone else you care about to stay alive.

## Janet Gets the Red Flag Warning

Here is an example of a warning from another type of outside source.

Janet had been receiving life insurance information for the past three weeks. Insurance sales people knocked at her door, phoned her night and day, and flooded her emails with information from their companies. In a session with me, I told her that it was a warning. I asked her if she and her husband had insurance policies. Janet said that she and her husband did have insurance, but her husband was planning to cancel the policies. I told her not to cancel the policies. Two months later, her husband was killed in a car accident. Had she canceled the life insurance policies, she would not have received financial help at her husband's death.

## Jim Gets a Well-Timed Message

Do you know that inanimate objects can also provide you with information and warning of the future? Let me tell you how a clock can offer a strong, significant message that speaks volumes. As a child, Jim often visited the home of his grandparents. He loved listening and watching an antique German cuckoo clock that hung on their living room wall. When the clock strikes the hours, it sounds like a common cuckoo's call that imitates the bird's name. It features a mechanical bird that emerges through a small trap door while the clock is striking each note.

After his grandparents died, he inherited the cuckoo clock. Needless to say, as an adult it held strong sentimental value because it was closely linked to his past and the memories of his loved ones. Jim was now a fifty-two-year-old bachelor. He considered himself to be a great catch, but no female was ever going to tell him what to do.

Jim lived in a comfortable home and his favorite clock still gave the correct time despite being covered with a thick layer of dust. The cuckoo clock could definitely use some tender loving care. In fact, his whole house could use some serious cleaning. However, instead of hiring a cleaning professional, Jim decided that it was cheaper to get a girlfriend.

When Jim initially met Sally, his eyes popped wide open and common sense went out the door. Sally was an attractive, thirty-two-year-old woman willing to "cook Jim's goose" if she got the chance. Sally definitely had plans for Jim so she moved in after a fast romance and "turned on the oven." Sally lost no time in taking control of the household. She was the first one to answer the phone when it rang and the first to open the door when someone knocked.

Sally cooked, cleaned, did the laundry, and removed cobwebs from the ceilings, but not from the cuckoo clock. She took it upon herself to rearrange the living room furniture and even disposed of some things that she felt were not appropriate. She jumped into Jim's car to run errands, go to the grocery store and the bank, without complaint. Of course, all of these "loving acts" gave her the opportunity to snoop around in his personal business and size up his financial status.

It was almost too good to be true for Jim, and it was. Sally was really into the rhythm of her scheming plans so one day she went through Jim's bedroom closet with a fine-toothed comb. She tossed out his old love letters and some of his clothes without mercy. Jim was upset by the invasion of his privacy but he kept it to himself until one fateful day. You could have heard a pin drop to the floor when Sally suggested that he toss out the cuckoo clock and replace it with something more modern.

Jim's heart sank to the pit of his stomach, but he was not going to give up his pride and joy under any circumstances. This began the first of many arguments about his taste in furnishings. Whenever the subject of the clock came up with Sally, a sudden case of diarrhea sent him running to the bathroom, but even then Jim did not put two and two together although the pattern was obvious and predictable.

Despite the clear warnings, Jim did not catch on to what was really happening until his beloved clock stopped working. Poor Jim was extremely puzzled. His prized cuckoo bird refused to come out of the clock. Jim felt very upset and angry. His gut-level feelings were yelling at him to run for cover, but he still ignored the forewarning. The clock had never stopped running prior to Sally's moving in with him. The cuckoo bird was sick and Jim felt ill because of his emotional link to it.

Finding a cuckoo clock doctor was frustrating, but he eventually found a repair shop that specialized in just cuckoo clocks. He reluctantly left it at the shop for several days for parts to be replaced. Jim felt like he was trapped in a cage like the cuckoo, with no control over his situation. However, he had a strong feeling that the solution was linked to the cuckoo clock. At last, Jim decided to seek help that would provide him with some answers. After a sleepless night, he scheduled an appointment with me to get my interpretation of the cuckoo bird's message.

I took a flash forward look into his future. Hmm, I thought. The word "cuckoo" is a major key word here. Since it was a clock, it was a strong indication of coming times. I zeroed in on the symbolism immediately because it was so obvious. I told Jim that the cuckoo clock's message was a warning that it was just a matter of time before his girlfriend would act crazy because of internal mental disorders, (greed and control issues). Their relationship was a done deal, and Jim would be unable to get Sally out of his house without taking drastic measures.

I told Jim that, if he did not get rid of Sally soon, his carefree bachelor days were over for good. Sally planned on clipping his wings and, like his cuckoo bird, he was not going to be able to fly from his coop without losing a few tail feathers. Jim laughed at my interpretation, but his gut feelings indicated that I was right, so he began to pay more attention to Sally's words and behavior. Close observation and listening gave him an "earful and an eyeful" when he finally removed his rose-colored lenses and mental ear-plugs.

In the meantime, Sally was getting more insanely jealous and controlling. At one point, she threatened to cut off Jim's testicles for talking to an old female friend on the telephone. That did it! This was the last straw of a negative chain of events. It actually acted as the ultimate catalyst to finally "wake up" Jim! He remembered my warnings and abruptly ended his relationship with Sally. However, this was not before she damaged two of his car tires, broke three windowpanes, kicked in his back door, and took a pair of scissors to the majority of his clothing. It was necessary to get police intervention and a restraining order before he finally got rid of Sally.

Jim eventually picked up his treasured cuckoo clock from the repair shop, and it worked better than ever. However, he was taking no chances so he never brought another woman to live in his home again. Jim made a costly mistake when he brought a girlfriend to live in his house to do the housework because he was too cheap to hire a cleaning service. Can you see how Jim's choices created his future problems? His negative experience was not the result of destiny or bad luck. Neither was he the victim of blind chance or random fate. His choices created his experiences. Jim should have seen that one coming and listened to the message that was loud and clear.

## Cynthia Learns the Value of Friendship

Here is another example of an inanimate object's giving a warning. Cynthia misplaced her house keys for the second time in three days. Cynthia was getting ready to go on a business trip, so she dismissed her forgetfulness as the result of having too much on her mind. Cynthia lived alone and considered herself to be very independent. Since her professional work involved a lot of traveling she did not take the time to acquaint herself with her next-door neighbors, and she had no pets. On the appointed day of her departure, she locked up her house and began the long trip to San Francisco.

After driving for a while, she decided to stop for lunch and gas up the car. When she reached for her purse to retrieve a credit card, she discovered that her house keys were missing once again. A sudden feeling of dread and apprehension (gut feeling) flooded her with alarm. She finally got the message that her subconscious was giving her a warning about her house in the form of her feelings and missing house keys.

Cynthia broke the record in getting back home only to find a brown pickup truck backed up in her driveway. Two suspicious-looking men were loading up her possessions in broad daylight. In disbelief, Cynthia phoned the police to report the robbery. When the police arrived, the thieves were stopped in their tracks by two strong officers prepared for a battle. Caught red-handed, the crooks dropped to the ground without a hassle. The burglars were taken immediately to jail and prosecuted. It turned out that Cynthia had shared information about going out of town with her hair dresser, who unknowingly passed the information to the thieves that robbed her. Guess what? Cynthia had remembered to lock her home after all! The crooks had used Cynthia's own backyard ladder to enter an unlocked second floor window. She later found her house keys in her tote bag instead of her purse.

Cynthia got the message. The best news is that Cynthia made friends with her neighbors. She adopted a large dog, Bertha, and hired a house sitter to watch her property when she was gone from home. Before every trip she locked all of her windows and even put the ladder in her garage. Needless to say, she never misplaced her house keys again or missed telling her neighbors goodbye when she left for any trip.

## Ed Never Got the Message

Sometimes warning messages are direct. A speeding ticket is a sign to slow down and observe driving regulations. It can save your life or the life of someone else. A stop sign is also an obvious sign to stop, look, and listen. Observing laws is a responsible act and a cheap price to pay for what might be your life. If you drive drunk, you will not need a psychic to predict the probable outcome.

How many times have you ignored signs only to suffer the consequences later? How much are you willing to risk in a gamble with death? I once had a client, Ed, who had two serious traffic accidents in a twelve-month period while under the influence of alcohol.

Ed never did get the warning messages, and now he does not drive at all. He cannot see his connection to the consequences of driving intoxicated. Ed lost his driving privileges to the California Department of Motor Vehicles, his mind to psychological blindness, and his ability to walk to a major traffic accident. Ed lost his money to lawsuits and DUI attorneys. Ed should have gotten it the first time that he was arrested for driving drunk. Prevention or a decision to ensure that he did not drive intoxicated would have changed the outcome. Ed's mind was paralyzed a long time before his body suffered the consequences of his fixed attitude.

## Ginger Escapes Death's Clutches

Here is another example of how your subconscious works to protect you from harm and warn you of possible future threats. Ginger was an attractive, wealthy widow in her middle sixties. She met Bill at a birthday party given by her co-worker. Bill was forty-five years old, handsome, witty, and charming. Ginger initially found Bill irresistible, but despite his charisma, there was something not quite right about him. She also felt a little uneasy about the difference in age, but after a whirlwind romance it was love at first sight! Soon after their meeting, Bill began leaving some of his clothing in her home, and eventually he moved in so smoothly that Ginger did not really know exactly when it happened.

A distracted mind is easily taken advantage of and controlled. At first, Ginger thought how nice it was to have a man around the house. Bill made himself useful by fixing leaky faucets, changing light bulbs, and mowing the lawn. He fixed a broken rotating fan and a lamp. However, when he attempted to fix the microwave oven it caught fire. After this incident, Ginger decided that it was cheaper to hire a professional electrician. Bill continued to be helpful in other ways. Why, he even brought in the mail. Of course getting the mail gave Bill the opportunity to also get an idea of her finances, bank accounts, etc. He asked her personal questions about everything, and Ginger, caught off-guard, sang like a canary.

Time passed and soon a more conniving side of his personality revealed itself. Mr. Fix-It was even slicker than the oil that he changed in her vehicle. Now Ginger was paying full attention! Bill was always snooping around her home and going through her paperwork. Bill also discouraged all outside communication with her family and friends. Just like that, their socializing days were over. When Ginger strongly objected, Bill explained that he was the jealous type and he wanted her all to himself. She began to feel very uncomfortable, suspicious, and apprehensive. All of her gut feelings were actually warning triggers from her subconscious that something was wrong. Ginger asked Bill to move out of her home. Bill refused to budge.

Every day she became more insistent that he leave. After another week of constant badgering, Ginger became even more uneasy and physically ill. When Ginger did not act on her initial feelings, her subconscious sent another warning that strongly indicated Bill's malicious intentions. In a vivid, terrifying dream, Ginger found herself in a portion of her garage that served as an improvised liquor bar. She watched as Bill poured poison from a small amber glass bottle into her bedtime hot toddy brandy. A human skull and crossbones on the label of the bottle warned of its contents. The nightmare was so right in her face that Bill might as well have pointed a loaded gun at her head.

Ginger finally got the red flag warning before she snapped. As soon as Bill went to the hardware store Ginger drove to the police department and reported her suspicions. Bill had several prior criminal incidents involving bullying older women and stealing from them. However, this was the first time he had resorted to poison to achieve his objectives. He was arrested and imprisoned.

Ginger's heart initially overruled her common sense. She should have paid attention to her physical senses and initial gut-level feelings. The early warnings were messages from her subconscious. It is never a good idea to invite people you do not really know into your home. Sometimes it is not a good idea even to invite people you do know well to live with you. Had Ginger ignored her dream, the cost could have been her life.

What have been some of your past premonitions or warnings? Did you act on them?

## CHAPTER TWO NOTES

# CHAPTER THREE

# Superstitions and Curses

M OST SUPERSTITIONS AND BELIEF in bad luck today began in ancient times. Human misinterpretation of various life experiences and unexpected events in nature created the fears that gave birth to superstition. People have always made strong efforts to invite good fortune and postpone bad luck. Knocking on wood when things are going well and keeping a low profile on Friday the 13th to avoid bad luck are just a couple of superstitions people still observe. Even if you do not believe in superstitions, do you sometimes go around ladders instead of walking under them?

You may think that you are modern and not superstitious, but your subconscious is the source of your primal fears. Different parts of the world are rich with traditions and household superstitions. For example, a dog that continues to howl can foretell the possible death of a sick family member in the home. If a broom falls down in a dwelling, an unwelcome guest may soon visit. Breaking a mirror can bring seven years of bad luck. No matter how foolish these customs and superstitions sound they still influence the reality of the person that believes in them.

At times your conscious mind cannot override your subconscious beliefs, fears, and superstitions. It will respond automatically to what it believes to be true and act on it. *Most superstitions have no reasonable explanation, but commonly accepted superstitions influence your behavior and have a major effect on your future.* Do you have any superstitions? Do you carry a good luck charm to ensure good fortune? What do you do to avoid bad fortune? The fears that lurk deep within your subconscious will always win over the logic of your conscious mind. Some superstitions are simply the fear of the unknown or a belief in luck or fate. Your superstitions may control your behavior and shape future experiences.

## Jodie's Beliefs are the Laws of Her Life

Your superstitions are connected to the past due to the beliefs and experiences of other people and your ancestors. Superstitions that have been passed down from generation to generation can still influence you to act on them. For example, my client Jodie told me that every time a black cat crossed her path she experienced bad luck, and she was right. When Jodie was a child, her mother told her that black cats always mean bad luck. Jodie's grandmother swore by this belief as well. Jodie, in turn, passed down her superstitions of black cats to her children who, in turn, will pass it down to their offspring.

*The fear of black cats has become a personal law for Jodie, and her subconscious is now programmed for bad luck. Jodie's subconscious is expecting bad luck when she sees a back cat so she will experience bad luck every time she sees one.* Black cats are not bad luck for everyone. However, if you *believe* that they bring bad luck, they will.

Be aware that your beliefs are the personal laws that you give your subconscious to act on. If you anticipate bad things to happen, then you will attract negativity because your subconscious obeys you. It is like a strong magnet pulling your future to you in the physical forms that you expect or anticipate. Can you see how what you expect to happen creates your experiences? When you make a prediction based on superstitions, you are allowing the past to influence you today.

Many ancient superstitions and symbols are based on simple chance events misinterpreted to apply to everyone. The fact is that bad luck symbols have nothing to do with you unless you have accepted these superstitions as trigger mechanisms in your subconscious. In this case, superstitions will produce exactly what you expect in your future because your beliefs are the laws of your life. These laws guide you consciously and unconsciously to make certain decisions and choices that create experiences. If superstitions are programmed into your subconscious, history will keep repeating itself until you replace superstitious beliefs with positive symbols and expectations. The following is an example of how superstitions create your future.

## Monica Ends Her Superstitions

A belief in fate, bad luck, and blind chance can lead to fear, doubt, and loss of control. Superstitious beliefs limit your conscious choices and the possibility of change in the present moment. For example, Monica, a well-to-do but superstitious widow, came to see me on her seventy-fourth birthday. Monica was wealthy due to her deceased husband's wise investments. Monica had postponed making a will because she believed that it was bad luck to tempt fate. Monica feared that, if she made her will, it might act as a signal to the Grim Reaper that she was ready to die. She also suspected that some of her family members were envious of her good fortune. Anything negative that she experienced she blamed on their wishing her bad luck. When Monica was involved in a three-car traffic crash, she blamed her relatives. When her dog Congo was killed by a car, she blamed her relatives. When Monica had a stroke, she blamed her relatives.

Needless to say, Monica did not want to leave her money to her alienated family members. Her relatives never phoned or visited her in the past, so Monica saw this as valid proof of her suspicions. Monica did receive one phone call from her cousin Sidney after suffering a stroke two years ago. However, when he found out that she had fully recovered, he hung up on her. I could tell that Monica's fears and superstitions weighed heavily in her mind. Monica very seldom left her home, and she had few friends. Monica had investments, money, and plenty of other assets, but no inner security.

When Monica came to my office I had her flash forward into the future to see the outcome if she died without a will. The outcome was quite predictable. Her greedy relatives would fight for her possessions, and probate would devour a large portion of her estate. With this in mind, I suggested that she create a living trust instead of a will. I advised her to give a small sum of money to her relatives to acknowledge them. Dissatisfied heirs would find the trust extremely difficult to contest. *In order for Monica's present circumstances to change, her attitude, beliefs, and superstitions had to change first in her mind.* I explained to Monica that superstitions have no power of their own. Monica's subconscious must first accept the superstitious beliefs as laws before they could produce her bad luck.

Once Monica was able to let go of some of her former superstitious beliefs and concerns, she was able to create a living trust to her satisfaction. When she took action by releasing her fears from her subconscious, she let go of procrastination and fears in her physical world as well. As soon as Monica was able to free herself from self-imposed limitations, she was able to start living again. Monica is now seventy-eight years old, and her mind is free of her earlier negative self-fulfilling prophecies. Being of sound mind, she could now spend all of her money on herself while she was still alive. Monica visited Spain last year, and this year she is planning a cruise to Alaska with her new beaux who is fifteen years younger than she is. Monica has no fear of being called a cougar. Growl!

**Curses and the Future**
You have heard that thoughts are things. Do you know that your thoughts are much more than the things you think about? They draw what you think in specific physical forms. This means that what you think about is the *cause* of physical things and future experiences. Everything that exists in the physical world is first a thought or idea that eventually takes form in your material world. As you think, your mind creates thought-forms to convey a complete idea, which suggests a particular outcome. For example, if someone hates you, their thoughts of you will contain certain negative mental and emotional suggestive images of you in some undesirable physical forms such as accidents or illnesses.

A telepathic thought suggests a particular physical outcome. These thoughts are emotionally charged and can be sent to another person with the speed of an arrow to its target. Direct hits and misses are determined by the intent and focus of the individual that is trying to pierce your energy field, or aura, with their negative intentions. Evil thoughts can be much more destructive than evil words because they are felt first as gut feelings before you are consciously aware of them. Although evil thoughts are not heard or seen, they zero in on their mark nonetheless.

The use of destructive thought-forms to harm another person is called a curse, a hex, or a whammy. You may associate a curse with a voodoo doll or a jinxed condition. However, you do not need a physical object to achieve a particular outcome. Curses are thought-forms made of negative energy and directed consciously or unconsciously at another person to do physical, mental, or emotional damage. You live in a sea of thought-forms all around you. Some are good and creative, and some are bad and destructive. Thoughts of anger, jealousy, and violence connect with each other to unite in a mental assault. When enough destructive thought forces are produced, they attack the unsuspecting victim, creating physical problems, accidents, and a host of other negative experiences that some people would call a curse.

Negative thoughts have a strong impact on your mood, behavior, and life. In fact, your attitude, daily life experiences, and health are all determined by your moment-to-moment thinking. For those of you that doubt this statement, the next time you are with an angry friend note how that person's negative emotions and attitudes affect your feelings. You can actually feel the bad vibes take over the individual, and you will have a strong desire to escape as your subconscious picks up on a possible physical threat to you and prepares you for fight or flight. Remember, the subconscious reacts to your thoughts and perception of events, and its job is to protect you at all cost. You may feel nauseous or anxious because the subconscious is directing your adrenal glands to action.

Intense arguments open the door to your subconscious, leaving it unprotected and receptive to negativity, which can be devastating. Anger, vengeance, violence, and other negative emotions can open you up to receive a host of problems in a heartbeat. Negative intentions sent to do harm to another person who is good and mentally protected will automatically rebound to the original sender. Your thoughts and words have a powerful effect on your future. They return like boomerangs as outcomes or the results of cause and effect.

Sometimes it is not easy to understand how your future is linked to your daily choices, thoughts, superstitions, and fears. However, there is a definite link between your mind, your physical body, and your life experiences. The following example can reveal how your emotions appear to curse you and create bad luck in your relationships and physical experiences.

## Ben and Connie's Domestic Wars

The battlegrounds of personal wars are in your own mind and within your own home. For example, Ben and Connie had a serious argument three days ago, but despite giving each other the cold shoulder, they both ignored the initial issue. Although angry words had not been yelled outwardly, they still existed as angry thoughts in their minds, as though they are a virus in the air waiting to attack them. The negative thoughts live in and around the couple as mental forms creating negative feelings such as anger, revenge, and hate. Although at this point they are only feelings, they are still the result of the couple's thoughts. If they continue to think about the things that create their feelings, these emotions will eventually manifest in their life experiences.

Once the negative thoughts are verbally expressed, they gain in strength by mixing with other destructive energy that already exists in their home. Thoughts of a like nature link together and make people bypass common sense because they lose control to their feelings. This makes it much easier to get into another argument. Arguments are very draining because people use up their energy to express their feelings emotionally. As long as the thought-forms exist, they are using the couple's energy to remain active or alive. Energy cannot be destroyed, so these mental images linger in the atmosphere of the couple, waiting to take physical forms.

Negative energy cannot be destroyed, but it can be changed into another form. Ben and Connie have to let go of the negative thoughts before the harmful energy can be transformed. The destructive energy of the thought-forms must be released or they will attract negative physical events or other problems in their future. Connie and Ben may never understand the original connection between their argument, negative mental energy, and their probable future accident, which is really the natural and predictable consequence of their unresolved, underlying issues. Winning round one, so to speak, does not bring closure to the overall battle, which will continue to manifest in other disputes or other destructive forces in their day-to-day lives.

# CHAPTER THREE NOTES

## CHAPTER FOUR
# Amulets, Charms and Talismans

C AN SOME SYMBOLS FORETELL BAD LUCK or predict good luck? Can today offer physical evidence or clues to tomorrow? Every culture around the world has its share of talismans, lucky charms, and amulets. Do you realize that you interact daily with symbols that trigger your mind and influence the way you feel, think, and conduct yourself consciously and unconsciously? Do not ridicule the use of talismans and lucky objects to influence your decisions and forecast your future. To do so is to under-estimate the power of the human mind to be influenced by things we touch, see, believe in, and share in the realm of our common experience. There is a belief found everywhere that some objects can protect, heal, offer good luck, and provide other beneficial influences due to the power of their suggestive value.

There is also a worldwide belief that certain things can bring bad luck and jinxes. The fear of the number thirteen, breaking a mirror, and count-ing the cars in a funeral procession can fill some people with the dread of attracting bad luck.

However, these symbols cannot bring you bad luck unless you believe that they will bring it. It is your belief in these symbols that draws negative influence to you. If your mind believes that bad luck is associated with these symbols, then it will deliver what it believes. The same thing holds true for lucky talismans, such as four-leaf clovers, rabbit feet, and horseshoes. Never underestimate the power of suggestion and belief.

## A Talisman

You may own a talisman without being aware of it. Your talisman could be a lucky coin that you always carry with you or perhaps a rosary draped around your rear view car mirror. A Saint Christopher car visor clip is another popular talisman for vehicles and their drivers. Whatever you believe in has suggestive value and will influence your choices and behavior. Some objects make us feel good because they hold sentimental value. For example, a talisman, such as your deceased grandmother's antique photo locket, attracts beneficial energies to you because it is charged with the energy of its owner and faith. The belief of its previous owner is embedded in the object itself. It is alive! It awakens your own faith and reconnects you to family members who may be gone, but not forgotten. This ancestral memory link makes you feel good or bad according to your past relationship with the previous owner.

Remember, objects hold the history of the person who owned them, including those passed down to future generations. Objects act as triggers to influence your subconscious according to what you believe about those objects.

## An Amulet

Some people wear amulets such as religious medals, crosses, and other blessed objects to ward off negative influences. If you wear a religious medal, you have an amulet. Many people with dangerous jobs wear a St. Michael's medal as an amulet of protection. In ancient times, it was common practice to honor heroes with prayers, offerings, and requests for help in all areas of life. Many people believe in cultural heroes with specific powers that can intervene in human problems to influence a particular outcome. The practice of devotion to the saints and honoring prophets is a long-standing tradition. Today, we ask the saints to intervene in our best interest and protect, heal, and guide us in our daily living. This ancient custom can be compared to asking family, friends, and deceased loved ones to pray for us when we have serious problems in modern times.

When we ask people to pray for us we experience peace of mind and inner strength to face life's many challenges united toward one goal. Prayers release our fears and allow the healing energy of both the living and the dead to lift us up above our burdens. Everything and everyone is interconnected. When we pray we link to the inner world of faith that is in us and all around us. Can you understand how some objects and people may influence your future because of what you believe regarding them? Do not ignore their significance.

## Joel's Beliefs Protect Him

Here is an example of how an amulet or religious medal was a beneficial influence to its owner. When Joel joined the US Army his Uncle Ned gave him a St. Michael's religious medal for protection. Military soldiers and other people in all walks of life wear amulets for protection, health, wealth, and other blessings. An amulet has a powerful suggestive value to the believer and is a constant reminder of its specific significance. Joel never removed the medal, and, in time, he developed great faith in its ability to protect him from harm. Every time he was in a dangerous situation, he touched the religious medal and asked the saint for protection. The power of positive suggestion reinforced his subconscious whenever he made physical contact, increasing his faith and trust. Joel attributed his four years of protection while in the military to his St. Michael's medal and he was right. Joel's confidence in his amulet to protect him created a strong trigger mechanism to remind him of its purpose. It influenced his daily decisions and made him think before he took unwarranted risk. Therefore, common sense also played an important roll in helping him keep safe and alive.

It is your faith in these objects that creates a protecting, beneficial influence and favorable circumstances. The power of your beliefs makes them effective tools in attracting what you believe. It is what your subconscious believes that will create your good or bad luck.

## Kenny Gets a New Lady Luck Talisman

Be aware that a belief in a talisman can also cause complete dependence on it. Kenny first came to see me when he lost his lucky talisman, an old coin that he always carried with him. The previous owner of the coin was his grandfather. His Grandpa Anthony swore to the coin's ability to bring good fortune, so he gave it to Kenny just before he died. Kenny did not have luck with women, but he did have one true love by the name of Lady Luck. As in all relationships, he did have to overlook some of her unpredictability. Sometimes, Lady Luck smiled down kindly on him, so despite his gambling losses, he counted his blessings and smiled back. Of course, Kenny believed that his Lady Luck talisman was the cause of his good fortune, and so it was. Kenny's luck began to change about one month after he lost his lucky talisman.

Kenny was desperate when he came to see me. I took a flash forward look into Kenny's future to see what would happen without his good luck talisman. If Kenny made no changes in his thinking, the forecast was indeed gloomy. There would be no good luck in his future. I explained to Kenny that it was the belief in the coin in his subconscious that brought him the good luck, not the coin itself. Kenny was programmed to believe in the luck of the coin, so it created his good fortune according to that belief.

The answer was to create another lucky coin so Kenny's subconscious could produce the good luck it anticipated. This was much easier said than done, but I finally convinced Kenny of the wisdom of my suggestion. The new lucky talisman offered the power of a new beginning and was a positive suggestion to his subconscious of good fortune. Kenny's new lucky coin would act as a trigger mechanism to remind him of its blessing influence.

Kenny now has another good luck talisman, and it's "hot." Every time that he rubs his new treasure it reminds him of its ability to bring good luck. Kenny was so happy with my advice that he called me his new Lady Luck. This is great as long as he does not rub me the wrong way.

## CHAPTER FOUR NOTES

CHAPTER FIVE

# Messages from the Plant World

YOU HAVE HEARD THE EXPRESSION, "Say it with flowers." A single rose can be a message of love. However, if it is not your birthday or another special occasion and you receive a big bouquet of flowers, it could invoke suspicion. Flowers can also be a means of asking for forgiveness and expressing caring. Flowers and plants have done our talking for us for a long time. In the Victorian period, emotions and feelings were not expressed openly, so receiving flowers became important symbolic messages to the happy recipients. The meaning of symbolic flower messages developed over time to communicate feelings that could not be expressed casually due to very formal and ritualized Victorian etiquette.

Today, do you realize that plants and flowers can offer another means of communicating important messages to you on a subconscious level? Of course, you must be able to interpret their clues to benefit from their messages of coming times.

Sometimes the universe gives you a negative message through nature to help you make the right choices or to change your perception of how you see things. Plants can be very significant *messages in disguise*, so do not ignore their importance as symbolic links to the future.

Mistakes can often offer explanations of something that is difficult for you to understand consciously because it is hidden beneath the surface. Train yourself to stop, look, and listen when something unusual occurs.

Messages come in many forms, and the plant world is just one source that will whisper or shout to get your attention. When something pushes your buttons, there is an important message for you, though it may not be obvious. Responding emotionally can make you lose control, and then you will miss the message entirely. Learn to read even negative messages from the plant world because they can help you change your future outlook. Many people, including me, talk to our plants. If you know how to listen, the plant world will speak to you.

## Mildred Says it with Flowers

Mildred placed an order for a dozen long-stemmed pink roses from her local florist shop. Mildred's niece was graduating from high school, and Mildred wanted to tell her congratulations with roses. Unfortunately, there was a mix up at the florist shop. Mildred was surprised when she answered the door and was handed a large bunch of snapdragon flowers. Before she could get over her shock, the florist truck drove away. After fuming for several minutes, Mildred decided to phone the florist shop and give them a piece of her mind. Of course, when you give someone a piece of your mind it drains you physically because your emotions use up your energy. Despite Mildred's frustration, she received a sincere apology, and the pink roses were soon delivered to the niece's address. Mildred was told that she could keep the snapdragons as an apology.

As a child, Mildred loved snapdragons because when she pinched open their mouths they would snap open and expose the "tongue and a scary face" inside the flower. As Mildred looked closer at the snapdragons she saw that the flowers' snout-like appearance looked even more like a dragon than usual. The flowers eventually died, but Mildred still could not get them out of her mind. Since she had experienced two other incidents with plant mix-ups recently, she made an appointment with me to discuss the matter. I told her that ordering roses for someone else but getting snapdragon flowers sent to her home by mistake indicated that there was definitely a message from the plant world trying to get her attention.

The message was obvious to me, but initially Mildred would not discuss the symbolism. She talked non-stop about incidental things. Since I could not get in a word edgewise, I pointed to the clock as a reminder to get down to business. There was complete silence, and then her mouth opened and closed just like a snapdragon. I knew Mildred had been keeping everything inside and would "snap" if she did not bring things out into the open. When she paused for a breath, I questioned her about what she thought the message of the snapdragons might be.

After beating around the bushes a few more minutes, Mildred finally admitted that in the last few weeks she had been upset and snapping at everyone. Why, Mildred even snapped at Jo-Jo, her pampered Persian cat. Jo-Jo was spoiled but sensible, so she completely avoided Mildred during this period of bewilderment. Jo-Jo came out from hiding under Mildred's bed only to eat her favorite gourmet meals. However, in the last two days, Mildred had the nerve to serve her dry, tasteless cat food. No way was Jo-Jo going to tolerate this injustice. Miss Jo-Jo showed her dissatisfaction with her mistress by pouting and pooping in the middle of Mildred's bed. Mildred told me that she thought she saw the cat smiling after it did its business. Thank God, Mildred could not be sure.

Mildred proceeded to tell me that in the past month she had experienced two other plant mix-ups. The second took place when she had ordered a Christmas cactus for her step-daughter Gina's birthday, but a mother-in-law's tongue was sent by "mistake." This plant (sansevieria) gets its name from its bitter taste and stiff upright leaves that contain a toxin that swells the tongue and throat if ingested. Normally, I would have connected the problem plant to her daughter-in-law, but since Mildred had never cared for her husband's daughter by a former marriage, the plant was definitely symbolic of her stiff, judgmental attitude and bitter disapproval of her step-daughter. Gina was the link and constant reminder of Mildred's husband's past history with another woman. It irritated her to no end so she constantly snapped at Gina.

The third flower mix-up happened when Mildred placed an order for a beautiful flower arrangement for her mother's ninetieth birthday. The flowers were beautiful, but when her mother opened the gift card, it read, *Sorry for the loss of your daughter.* The gift card was a mix-up, but its message was loud and clear. It was definitely a warning! Mildred was beginning to take notice. At this point, Mildred had to get in touch with what her subconscious was telling her, and she had to let go of her jealousy, anger, and resentment issues.

I had Mildred flash forward into the probable future to tell me what she saw if she made no changes in her attitude. Mildred told me that if she did not change her attitude, bitterness would damage her body and her emotions would agitate her mind. Her bitter words and thoughts would eventually create serious physical and mental health issues. All of the flower mix-ups were direct warnings to Mildred to let go of her control and anger issues. Mildred could make other choices and she did so.

Within three weeks of our intuitive session, Mildred made up her mind to change her probable future by changing her thinking through reprogramming. Within one month, she apologized to her step-daughter for her past rude behavior. Mildred was now happily included at all family functions. On another note, Jo-Jo assumed her old habit of sleeping in the middle of Mildred's bed instead of under it. Jo-Jo kept one eye open, and was ready to act to protect her interest. Of course, Jo-Jo thought that she was the one that had whipped Mildred into shape. In the event that Mildred misbehaved again, Jo-Jo knew exactly what to do.

## CHAPTER FIVE NOTES

# CHAPTER SIX

# Warnings from Nature

E VERYTHING IN NATURE HAS SOMETHING to tell you personally if you listen. Information comes to you in many forms and from many sources. You are connected to your environment, the elements, seasons, animals, minerals, and plants. You are a part of the stars in the sky, the sun, moon, oceans, and mountains. There is absolutely nothing that you are not connected to. Some warnings can easily be missed if you cannot see your connection to nature. Nature constantly sends you messages that you may ignore unless they are dramatic. Stop, look, and listen carefully because, if a whisper is not heard, nature's voice will follow through with a loud shout.

To make a point, nature may step in with major storms, tsunamis, earthquakes, and hurricanes to get your undivided attention. Nature sends its warning messages when thunder roars and lightning strikes. Failing to recognize early warning signs indicates that you are out of tune with Mother Earth. The following information can help you understand the power of your thoughts and your inner-connection with nature because they are inseparable.

## Your Connection to Nature

Nature reveals that everything is inter-connected, inter-related, and linked to the very core of our existence. To understand this connection you must realize that there is only one Universal Spirit that unites all great nations and our global environment. This Universal Heart branches out from its spiritual center to all nations despite our physical differences and locations. Your ability to understand this inner-connection to all life is rooted deeply within you. At this time, the rhythm of its spiritual heartbeat is being felt all around the planet without discrimination. It is causing us to shift our perspectives from a personal point of view to a global awakening. This requires us to transform our thinking before we can experience a global healing in our physical world. Only great change within each individual can initiate personal and planetary evolution. You must recognize this connection to change the future.

We have all collectively created the world in which we live because nature is interconnected through our subconscious. Everything within our mind is also interconnected to our physical environment, including the animals, plants, and minerals. This may sound like a mind-boggling idea because we do not realize that our subconscious is the connecting link between nature and our material world. There is a definite interconnection between our thinking and our physical world. When the balance of nature is upset by human misuse, greed, hatred, and violent behavior, the negative mental imagery is automatically duplicated or re-sent to us in the physical forms of earthquakes, hurricanes, tsunamis, and other worldwide catastrophes.

The collective emotional disturbance in our human minds is automatically returned by nature on a universal level in our material world in the physical forms of epidemics, plagues of violence, wars, economic failures, and so on. When nature gets fed up with our negativity it automatically sends it back to us in a physical forms like a boomerang. There is no mistaking the universal law of cause and effect when Nature takes action. The bible refers to this law as "You reap what you sow." In other words, the seeds that you plant in the soil of your subconscious will reproduce in your physical world as effects.

This law is also recognized as the law of balance and compensation. If you believe that everything is interconnected, can you see the relationship of your thoughts to your environment? Nature is connected to you through your subconscious, so be careful how you use nature to predict your future. The law of attraction will act like a magnet pulling your thoughts to bless or curse you in the future. Ignorance of the law does not excuse you from the consequences of wrong thinking. The universal law of cause and effect will be discussed in a later chapter. In the meantime, be careful of how you use nature in your words and thoughts. Never swear by nature or other forces in your thoughts or with your words.

## Toby Attracts Lightning

Here is an example of how Toby's thinking and wrong choice of words became a self-fulfilling prophecy as they were reproduced and automatically sent back to him by nature. Toby came to see me after a series of accidents. He was a pleasant seventy-two-year-old man, and he had the habit of saying, "If I am telling a lie, may I be struck dead by lightning," This statement was repeated at least three times in our intuitive session. I told Toby that he was asking for death from nature by lightning. Toby told me that he avoided thunderstorms and he never messed with electricity, so he was safe.

I was still not satisfied with his answer, so I explained that electricity comes in many forms. I knew that I was on the right track after questioning Toby further about his accidents. Toby told me that he had recently suffered an electrical shock when he tried to remove a burnt piece of bread from his toaster with a fork without unplugging it first. Toby experienced a more serious shock while changing a light bulb in the oven of his kitchen stove. Toby had used a wet cloth to remove the electric oven light because the old bulb was still hot. The third incident occurred when he was cutting off some of the branches of a large tree that was too close to the roof of his house. While standing on his roof top, Toby tripped over the electrical cord and fell twenty feet to the ground, breaking his left foot.

I took a flash forward look into Toby's future. Yikes! I told Toby that the universe was sending him strong warnings that if he continued to swear by lightning, he would physically, emotionally, and mentally plug into it. Toby's thoughts and words would eventually take physical form and destroy him. Toby told me that he was sure that his "accidents" were only coincidences. I believe that he did try to stop his negative self-prophecy, but by then it was too late. Toby was killed three months later. Toby was wrong when he told me that he would not be struck dead by lightning. Toby was killed indirectly by lightning. A large tree in front of his bedroom's patio glass door was struck by lightning during a bad electrical storm. The heavy tree crashed through the glass door and landed on top of Toby, crushing him to death. It is unfortunate that Toby died. He was a good man and I still remember him in my prayers.

## CHAPTER SIX NOTES

# CHAPTER SEVEN

# Your Body Can Predict Illness

Y OU CAN RESET YOUR SUBCONSCIOUS BODY CLOCK to run healthier and stay well. Your subconscious protects you and gets its message across using your gut-level feelings, dreams, omens, nature, symbols, and pain. Pain is a physical symptom or sign of an area that needs your full attention. Recognizing the connection between your mental attitude and physical illness will provide you with a major source of information that may save your life. Your physical body is a feedback system for your mind. All conditions are the physical evidence of the body/mind relationship and its connections to everything. You must stop blaming your age for all of your problems and health issues. Your subconscious does not know how old you are or care if your biological clock is still ticking.

If you are unhealthy, perhaps you need to reexamine your beliefs to determine how past programming may be influencing your health today. Your body provides clues and answers about your mental attitude, your emotions, and your health or lack of it. Specific parts of your body have symbolic meaning. Paying attention to how your physical body talks to you is very beneficial and revealing. A sore throat may be a sign of problems in self-expression or anger in communicating. A stomachache may indicate a loss of power and control if it is felt in the solar plexus area. Primal instinct talks to you through your feelings that you cannot always put into words. If you have a lot of stomach problems, here is a simple question to ask yourself: what or whom can't I stomach? A headache could mean that you must release your mental burdens. Your conscious mind must do the letting go or release work.

If you are in touch with your body's language, health issues will reveal the areas on which you need to start working. If you procrastinate, you will not be able to take preventive actions before illness occurs. Of course, you may have real physical issues, but always try to find a mental link to your physical body and health concerns. Paying attention to your physical body can definitely give you signs of future health issues. When your mind and physical body do not see eye to eye, there is a disconnection, so the subconscious will try to talk to you through your body. A warning of things yet to come can help you make the right health decisions today.

Psychosomatic medicine tells us that many illnesses are mentally self-induced. Many physicians believe there is a definite connection between illness and stress because of the body/mind link. In fact, some illnesses can be predicted based on the amount of stress in one's life. The holistic approach to healing maintains that all aspects of a person must be considered for effective treatment to the whole being. This includes the psychological, physical, and social needs. Spiritually is also considered an integral part of the whole person. Your thoughts and your feelings affect your health and behavior, creating your future experiences. Medical scientists have found that the conscious mind can be taught to control and influence the heart beat, muscular tension, and blood pressure through bio-feedback. When you let go of your negative emotions on a mental level, you also let them go on a physical level and your healing is automatic.

Since we are all interconnected on an emotional level you can see that what we think, refuse to let go of, or forgive in our minds produces illness in our physical bodies and affects all of us. This gives a new meaning to *body language*, doesn't it? In this case, body language is the language of feelings or emotions of which we are all a part, whether we are human beings, animals, plants, or even rocks. When you cannot see the connection you will have to feel it somewhere in your physical body or life experiences. Perhaps all physical illness cannot be avoided since our knowledge of science is limited. But our physical and mental health will be improved as we honor the connection between the two.

## Letting Go is Healing

Your conscious mind is the boss; it gives the orders and is responsible for what goes into your subconscious. The subconscious is the servant; it accepts the orders and is responsible for what goes out in your physical world. Your subconscious does not know how to let go of negative mental baggage after accepting it. It can be difficult to release something when you do not recognize the necessity of letting go. The fight-or-flight response of the subconscious is instinctive, but the order to "release" must be purposely summoned by the conscious mind before the subconscious can obey and let go mentally, emotionally, and physically. If you are in a dangerous situation, being on high alert can be helpful if you must fight or flee. However, when adrenaline is not used up by action, it creates stress hormones, which are mental poisons to the physical body.

The body and mind are connected and must *work together* to be successful teammates. The word *release* means to let go, to forgive, or to give up. When you release something in your mind, you also release the cause of what you are experiencing in your physical body or life experiences, which are the effects or outcomes in your physical world.

## The Body and Mind Connection

You must learn to connect whatever health problems you may be experiencing to what you are refusing to release in your mind because your thoughts are linked to your emotions. When you refuse to forgive, your subconscious cannot release the negative emotions that are stored in your physical body. Your emotions affect all of your cells. If you hold hate or resentment in your mind, it will cause illness, stress, or other negative conditions. Your internal "emotional health" will manifest itself in the external "physical health" of your body.

Your body talks to you in the form of physical signs and symptoms in connection with your thoughts and emotions. For example, if you are continually "pissed off" at everything, the outcome of your inability to let go of your attitude may eventually result in a urinary tract infection. Your body parts are connected to your thoughts, attitudes and feelings.

A urinary infection or an obstruction in the flow of urine may indicate that you must let go of a mental obstruction in your mind first before your body can get back into the "flow" of healing.

When you find out that you have a health issue, start thinking right away about what might be the mental cause of your condition. Health issues force you to pay attention to what your body is saying. Letting go is nearly always the solution. This is especially true if you have release issues.

## Cecilia Gets a Second Chance

Cecilia came to see me after she was diagnosed with a serious illness. She was an attractive, well-dressed, thirty-two-year-old woman, but she was very uptight. She was going through some serious health issues, so I understood her anxiety. However, if I were going to help her, I needed to find the link between her thinking and her present health predicament.

She was at a serious turning point. I questioned her about what was going on in her life in the last year or so. Cecilia told me that her husband of three years had left her for another man a year earlier. Cecilia was shocked and devastated. She had no idea of her husband's sexual preference. She felt bitter, angry, and betrayed. I could see that just talking about the situation pushed her buttons as if it had happened yesterday. When you recall an event your subconscious also reconnects you to your feelings at the time. If Cecilia did not mentally let go of her destructive emotions, the unreleased stress hormones would continue to destroy her body.

Yesterday's choices must be dismissed from your mind today, or they will continue to make you feel like a victim of circumstances. A detached observation will let you know that your only connection to the past is mental. Of course the body bears witness to the past as well, with scars and aging. But the habit of picking at open wounds must be curbed so that healing can take place for overall heath of mind and body to be maintained. If you let go in your mind, you will automatically let go of the emotions in your physical body. Do not identify yourself with the mistakes of your past. Forgive and forget your past mistakes and yesterday's choices. Guilt and regret are experienced when you try to punish yourself today for the mistakes you made years ago. To forgive means you must release self-blame or your body and life experiences will be the payback. The best method of predicting your future is to observe your moment-to-moment experiences and consciously let go of destructive self-recrimination thinking that is making you sick and afraid of your future. There is much value in self-study. You can then learn about life experiences from the world's greatest teacher, life itself.

I began with a short meditation to help Cecilia relax. I took a flash forward look into Cecilia's future. If she were unable to release the cause of her illness the outcome could be very serious. I saw that, after months of resentment and animosity toward her husband, she had become very bitter and destructive. She started drinking and blaming fate for her circumstances. It was obvious that the real culprit was her inability to forgive. It was both the mental cause of her disease and the consequence of not letting go.

Cecilia was a good person, but she had a few skeletons in her closet and she wanted to keep them there. A few months earlier she had been involved in a serious accident when she drove intoxicated. Guilt made Cecilia think that God was punishing her for causing the accident. Guilt and illnesses are usually not connected to self-punishment and accidents, but they can be the result of self-blame.

The subconscious is programmed to be the final judge of your character and conduct. If you feel remorseful for something you did, even decades ago, your subconscious will take this as an accusation and will punish you for wrong-doing. Some people may not believe that negative thinking influences us to make negative choices, but it's true. Illness related to mental factors, such as stress, resentment, and regret, is the outcome when we refuse to change our attitudes. You mental state affects your physical health through the body/mind connection. You also have a direct energy link to the people that you love and hate. You can sometimes feel their emotions and state of mind.

Along with Cecilia's medical care, she had to change her attitude. I suggested professional counseling and therapy. Cecilia had to let go in her mind to release what was tormenting her and making her sick. Self-forgiveness is just as important as forgiving other people because it releases the mental toxins that are physically poisoning you. The subconscious is the same powerful energy source that heals your body, but you are required to forgive and let go of your negative emotions before the subconscious can perform its healing function.

Forgiveness is not always instantaneous. It is most often a gradual process of letting go of a past debt that you believe someone owes you. When you feel abused and betrayed, forgiveness is not usually the first thing that comes to your mind. Before you can forgive others, you must deal with your own anger, resentment, disappointment, and pain. Painful memories can keep you locked in the past and hold you hostage today. Forgiving others and self-forgiveness releases you from judgment and brings peace to your mind. Peace comes from the inside out rather than from external sources. Forgiveness undeniably increases your ability to heal, maintain health, and let go of internal feelings that cause stress.

Eventually, Cecilia was able to release her inner enemies from the inside, where they began, and she experienced a complete healing. Time heals, but does not forget or forgive without a *mental release*. Despite her initial trust issues, in due time, Cecilia remarried and enjoyed her new life with a wonderful man and their two children.

## Intervention Can Change the Future

The best method of promoting good health is preventing illness. If you are feeling physically ill or emotionally out of control, perhaps you need to reexamine your thinking to determine how past programming may be influencing your health. You can do nothing about the past because it has already happened, but future events have not yet occurred, so it is possible to alter them if you pay attention to existing conditions or warning signs. Future events that are distant in time are easier to change because there may be many intervening actions to take before the future event plays out.

Do you know that your subconscious is always working to protect you and keep you healthy? One of its jobs is to warn you of future health issues. Pain and illness are sometimes strong indications from the subconscious that something is wrong in your thinking. Sometimes there are no physical warnings. If the subconscious cannot get its message to the conscious level, it will try to communicate to you in omens, symbols, nature, accidents, illnesses, and even your dreams.

## Lola's Dream Saves her

Lola once told me of a vivid dream in which she was choking. In her dream, she helplessly watched as her face turned beet red and her eyes began to water. Her nose was filled with mucus, and she began coughing so badly that it became difficult to swallow. She woke up in a panic. Lola spent a sleepless night before talking with me the next morning. When she told me about her nightmare, I advised her to go to the doctor immediately. Lola lost no time getting a medical check-up, which found a serious throat disease. Early detection and surgery saved her life because she did not procrastinate about seeing her physician. The dream had definitely been a strong warning from her subconscious.

Trust in your dreams and your intuition. Pay attention to how your physical body talks to you because it could be critical that you listen and act immediately.

## Ben Got the Message Loud and Clear

Ben was a chain smoker. He had smoked two to three packs a day since he was seventeen years old. He was now sixty-two, and he did not intend to quit. Until his dream, that is. One night Ben had a nightmare that scared him into quitting smoking. When he visited me, I asked him how he had quit smoking so quickly. Ben said that God appeared to him in his dream and told him that if he did not stop smoking he would die shortly. Ben was highly motivated. Ben never had another cigarette from that day forward. Ben changed his fate by changing his thinking. He stopped smoking cold turkey because he did not want cigarettes to gobble him up.

## Andrea Learns the Power of Intervention

Foreknowledge of a coming health issue based on existing knowledge can intervene with a future medical diagnosis. Andrea finds Mrs. Field's cookies and See's Candies irresistible. All sweets make her drool and drive her wild with desire. The only problem is that Andrea is a borderline diabetic with a family history of diabetes. Andrea can flash forward into the future to see the probable outcome if she continues to eat sweets at her current rate. If Andrea makes no changes in her thinking and diet choices today, she could develop Type-2 diabetes.

Andrea must become conscious of her thinking and everyday food choices, which have become habits. She must learn to read food labels before she gobbles up goodies like the Cookie Monster, not afterward. Sugar comes in many forms, and many starches turn to sugar after they are digested. Andrea must watch out for white breads, some fruits such as bananas, white rice, and potatoes, to name but a few forms that can raise blood sugar levels. If Andrea can release the food temptations from her mind, she will be able to intervene before she develops the disease. Andrea can also begin walking, working out, or dancing to improve her health.

Andrea can change her future by changing her thinking and eating habits today. She can also look into the health history of her family tree to review other common health issues. We are not fated to inherit all of our family's medical problems. Many of our so-called inherited health conditions are simply the outcome of lifestyle choices. A family that is big on eating starches and sweets has a greater tendency to develop Type-2 diabetes. We have many options, and they all began in our thinking and our choices today. Healthy choices will definitely give Andrea some control over her diabetes tendency. Awareness must be followed through with intervening action to control some of her health problems.

Are you concerned about future health issues? What are some of the things that you are experiencing now? Is stress an issue? What about your weight and lifestyle choices? What are some of the negative influences in your life now? What or who has the power to sway your thinking or your choices? What encourages you to make unhealthy decisions? Are you allowing a person, place, or thing to determine your future? Think seriously.

Sometimes being under the influence has nothing to do with drugs or alcohol. Learn to say no to temptations that take your body, mind, and emotions out of your control. Saying no to negative influences is a healthy choice if you want to live to see the future.

Keep your mind healthy and your body strong. Inner strength will outlast physical strength every time. Do some form of exercise even it is only walking around the shopping mall. Try meditating and praying to help you release what is not for your highest good. Use affirmations to keep your mind and body working toward the same goals. Do not put off making an appointment to see your doctor on a regular basis. Act now and you can prevent at least some stress-related illnesses. Do not wait until you are dying to see your physician. Of course, if your doctor is ignoring your serious symptoms, change doctors fast.

What are the preventive measures that you can take now to avoid physical, mental, or emotional problems in the future? Take a few minutes to predict how you can intervene to create a healthier future.

# CHAPTER SEVEN NOTES

## CHAPTER EIGHT

# Intervention Can Change an Outcome

THINKING ABOUT YOUR FUTURE requires you to be aware of what is happening in the present. You should always remind yourself that the connection between the past and the future is today. You can consider some probable outcomes and disregard some things that are not likely to happen. You can make the most of coming times if you watch your physical world for signals and warnings of coming times. What patterns are you creating for future experiences? Project yourself into your own future and see what awaits you if you do nothing about your present circumstances to shape your future.

Do not fear your future. Use common sense, make the right choices, and there will be no surprises. You will no longer fear being the victim of life's circumstances. Plan and prepare for the future now. Today is all that you have, so you must decide what you can do now to change future circumstances.

### Kellie Learns to Play a Different Role

Kellie was a popular model and actress. She was sought out by many magazines to do cover photos all over the world. She even received some recognition for various roles she played in the movies. Every penny that she made went to purchase costly jewelry, expensive clothes, fast cars, and gigantic houses. Cruise ships and jet planes took her to far-off lands and exciting places. Time marched on.

Around age thirty-five, Kellie noticed some tiny crows' feet around her eyes. At forty-five, she noticed a few more significant changes in her face and body, a little sag here, and bigger sag there. At about fifty-five, she noticed the whole crow's foot; it had spread, and it was enormous. Since she had lots of money, she paid famous plastic surgeons to lift it up, cut it off, suck it out, and stuff it. Face lifts, liposuction, and Botox injections were not cheap, but she could afford them as long as she kept working. She spent a lot of time looking into a large magnifying mirror that revealed every flaw.

Time moved forward, and soon no new offers of work were coming her way. It was time to withdraw from the public eye. She became moody and critical of the movie industry. When she first came to see me, she wore a beautiful, well-tailored suit, giant sunglasses, a large hat, and gloves. (This was the 1960s.) A flash forward look into her future in earlier times would have helped her plan so that she could take intervening actions to prepare for getting older. However, all that she had was today.

I recommended her to audition for other acting roles that fit her present age category and to start saving money. Kellie still had talents and beauty even if she did not have youth. "Make the best of what you have," was my advice. She left humbled, but she was standing tall. She did not remove her sunglasses during our session, but she did remove her hat and gloves. After she left I spent fifteen minutes looking into a magnifying mirror. I did not believe the mirror because all it did was make mountains out of molehills. The next day I purchased larger sunglasses.

### Fred Plans Ahead

Fred is aware that another corporation has just purchased the company that employs him. The new company is bringing in its own people in three months. Now would be the time for Fred to start looking for other employment. By planning ahead, he is preparing himself for the future he wants.

If you are aware of the direction in which you are headed, you can predict the future to some extent. You can examine your potential future and determine the probable outcome of some events before they occur. When you flash forward, you can foresee the future clearly and powerfully. You can then make the necessary changes in the present time. Training your conscious mind to bypass the doubt and disbelief of the subconscious will increase your control over future events. Common sense and intuition can then predict the outcome.

**Joseph Plans for his Future**

Joseph initially came to see me because he was ready to move to the next level at work. I asked Joseph what his short-term goals were. He told me that he needed more money because he and his wife were seriously considering starting a family. Joseph's present position did not provide enough medical insurance to cover this expense. With this goal in mind, I had Joseph take a flash forward look into his future. Joseph had to see the outcome of what he wanted before he took the necessary steps to get there. By looking and thinking ahead, he was able to prepare for his goal.

Joseph knew that the present office manager was to retire in four months. If Joseph could pass the work requirements this would greatly increase his chances for the position. I told Joseph to start preparing now and attend whatever classes he needed to accomplish his goals. Although the pay increase would not raise his income greatly, there would be other fringe benefits, such as a yearly bonus, an IRA fund, and better medical insurance coverage. By paying attention, Joseph was able to flash forward into his future and come to a logical conclusion from an established tendency already set in motion. Your future consists of a sequence of continuous probabilities influenced by your choices today. Today, Joseph is the office manager and the proud father of twin boys.

## CHAPTER EIGHT NOTES

# CHAPTER NINE
# Self-Fulfilling Prophecy

THE HUMAN MIND IS CAPABLE of foresight if it is not distracted. You can train yourself to look into future possibilities by daily observing your own thinking, choices, and life experiences. You are capable of accomplishing remarkable achievements, but you must first overcome self-imposed limitations. You are required to remove your rose-colored glasses. Your subconscious is programmed to interpret your life according to your past perceptions. Therefore, your mind and beliefs can establish opportunities or boundaries, freedom or roadblocks.

Be particularly aware of self-fulfilling prophecies. Your thoughts are linked to you physically, mentally, and emotionally. If you make a prediction for yourself consciously or subconsciously, you will cause it to become true. What is your daily self-talk? The words and thoughts you say and think today will come home like chickens to roost tomorrow.

Knowing what you can expect in coming times can be comforting and offer peace of mind to those of you that prepare for the future today. If you begin to connect your future with your current choices you will see that your future is always changing because it is adaptable. Every time you change your mind, you change your future. What are you predicting for yourself? Negative thinking will reveal itself in your daily experiences as problems, health issues, and accidents. Your foreseeable troubles must be resolved in your mind where they began, or they will continue to surface in your life in various disguises as surprises or fate.

Here is some great news. All that you change in your thinking also changes the conditions in your outside world. When you do not understand your inner world, your outer experiences may appear to be meaningless and unrelated. Look at your day-to-day experiences. What is the universe telling you? Continued failure, bad luck, heartache, and other negatives are messages that you need to make inner changes in your thinking. Do not try to find solutions on the outside. Look beneath the surface of what you are experiencing. Question your point of view from every angle. Be honest with yourself. Review your daily experiences to get a glimpse into your future. If you are aware of what you are thinking today, you will have a good idea of what you can expect tomorrow.

In a self-fulfilling prophecy, our choices do not usually result in death, so our daily decisions are not perceived as life-threatening. Instead we get the result of our choices. That is why we need to make the connection between our daily choices and future experiences. Every time that you make a choice, you experience the result. Get in touch with what your gut-level feeling is telling you about your decisions. Use common sense before making a final choice.

Your daily living is full of previews of coming attractions that you must learn to recognize. Do you want to see your future today? You can by observing and connecting your words and thoughts to your everyday physical experiences. Are you blessing or cursing yourself? The following examples will give you an idea of how self-fulfilling prophecies work and become your future experiences. Can you identify with them?

## Maureen Needs an Attitude Adjustment

Before Maureen went to sleep, she was thinking of all her problems. Her car payment was due, and she was already late with the rent. She had just received her second driving ticket in five months. She also had a demanding new boss who actually expected her to work. Maureen woke up in a terrible mood, not realizing that by going over and over in her mind all of her troubles she was actually programming herself for more problems. She expected more bad things to happen, and they did.

In the morning her hot water tank went out and produced only a cold shower. She had no cream for her morning cup of coffee. When she slammed down her coffee mug, it broke. She forgot to let her dog out so it had an accident on the carpet. Maureen left late for work and ran out of gas. When she called to report that she would be late for work, the new boss told her that she did not have to come in at all. It was one negative thing after another. Maureen's whole day was influenced by her thinking and expectations because her subconscious made the negative prophecy come true.

## Paul Lets Go of Self-Defeating Triggers

You must avoid negative self-fulfilling prophecies in your daily verbal expressions and thoughts that can send you spiraling into a dark vortex of despair. Even a picture hanging on your wall can trigger a sense of hope-lessness and depression if you connect it with something that makes you feel sad. Be aware of self-defeating triggers that keep you locked into the past with words, songs, text messages, movies, letters, emails, or greeting cards. Be aware of how a flashback can keep you locked in the past. Here is an example of how memories control your future and a negative self-ful-filling prophecy waits to sabotage you.

Paul came to see me when his girlfriend Mona had left him for another woman seven months earlier. Before Mona ended their three-year rela-tionship, she told Paul that she had to find herself, and that was that. When Paul initially visited me, he walked with a crutch and his shaved head had several cuts and bruises. His left arm was in a cast, and he actually groaned when he sat down. When I asked Paul what had happened, he told me that he had been in three accidents within six months and the last accident happened just a week before his appointment with me.

The first accident happened when a car hit him while he was jaywalk-ing. Paul said that he was "lucky" because he only broke one leg. The second accident happened when he fell down a flight of stairs. Paul said that he was "lucky," because he only broke one arm. The third accident happened when he used his crutch to reach a high kitchen shelf to get down a glass jar of peaches. The glass jar shattered when he tried to stop it from falling with his *head*. Once again, Paul said that he was "still lucky" because the shattered glass could have blinded him. I asked Paul if he had a death wish. He said that he had been feeling very depressed. I questioned Paul about what he had been doing before the accidents. He replied that he had been looking at photos of his old girlfriend while listening to their favorite love songs. Paul was also reading old love letters and greeting cards that he had received from Mona in happier times.

When you want to forget someone or something, do not keep looking and listening to reminders that keep you tied to the past. Mona was now long gone, but Paul felt he could not come to terms with his loss. In fact, Paul told me several times in our session that he did not want to continue living without her. I told Paul that his negative energy was like a magnet pulling death toward him. If he continued to wish that he were dead, his subconscious would see that he got his wish. Paul's negative attitude attracted the car accident, the fall down the stairs, and the glass jar's breaking on his head. His subconscious accepted his conscious orders as laws and then made them happen.

I had Paul flash forward to look into his future and tell me what he saw. He told me that if he continued his self-fulfilling prophecy, he would eventually attract his death. After some serious soul searching, he started to shed tears. He said that he really wanted to live, but he wanted the quality of his life to get better. It was time for Paul to let go of his self-defeating physical and mental triggers. The first thing I suggested to Paul was to move from his old apartment, stop listening to old love songs, get rid of old love letters, and stop looking at old photos of Mona. This would help him to let go of the physical reminders of the past. However, mental and emotional attachments required letting go in his mind and heart.

I suggested therapy to start his healing process. Paul needed to reprogram his subconscious to move forward in life. Paul was only thirty-four years old, and if he wanted to live to be thirty-five, he had to break his death wish. Paul needed to keep his mind busy and his body active. I suggested he pursue kickboxing more seriously because he was already interested in it. I also advised Paul not to kick Mona to the curb when she returned to ask him for a second chance. I was kidding, but I was right!

A year later, Mona showed up and wanted to resume the relationship, but Paul was not interested. He was now a happily married man with a baby on the way. Paul told Mona that he had found himself and that was that.

## Things to Think About

Past programming can interfere with our future experiences. Our thoughts are suggestive, and our gut-level feelings come from our subconscious that is linked to our past memories. Things that happened to us years ago may interfere with our logic and reasoning mind today. We are still emotionally programmed by our past negative experiences, which can be triggered by persons, places, and things that recall the emotions linked to a particular event.

Is a past trauma interfering with your ability to live fully today? What you think or believe creates how you feel, which guides your behavior and moods to influence your choices. If you cannot control some of your emotional response today, your gut-level feelings may not be dependable or accurate in current situations. Gut-level feelings are sometimes based on internal clues that you don't always identify. A strong feeling to act can be perceived from rapid cognition or heightened sensory awareness from the environment. Occasionally it is drawn from internal signals. So, can a strong hunch prove to be accurate? Absolutely! The people that decided not to go to work on 9/11 were tuned into their internal body signals. Sometimes it is difficult to distinguish between rapid understanding and authentic gut-level feelings. Even experts disagree on the differences. Paying attention to internal and external signals can help you recognize the difference and then you can come to your own conclusions about a possible outcome.

Your negative thoughts, words, and actions attract your future experiences like an inescapable nightmare. What are some of your self-fulfilling prophecies? Learn to review your past predicaments to see if you can discover the link between your choices and personal crises. How were you caught off-guard or unprepared? When catastrophe struck, what was on your mind? Did any of your earlier experiences hint at the future, though you ignored the warning? When you fell down the flight of stairs, what was on your mind? Were you stressed out, mad, depressed, or worried? Most people do not relate physical accidents with their state of mind or feelings. If you understand that everything is inter-connected, you will see the relationship between your thoughts and your outer experiences. Your self-fulfilling prophecies will come true because you will consciously or subconsciously make choices that will cause the event to happen.

Be aware that your self-fulfilling prophecies can be blessings or curses depending on how you use your thoughts and words. What have you been experiencing recently? Are you constantly being passed over at your employment? Would you like to change jobs or end relationships? Would you like to begin something new? What are your expectations? What are your beliefs on money, power, relationships, happiness, healing, security, employment, etc? What do you constantly tell yourself about these areas? Do you count your blessings but curse your fate? Your words and thoughts should only be used to heal, to bless, and to benefit humanity. One method of changing old programming is to imprint your subconscious by auto-suggestions or affirmations. Read the chapter, The Power of Affirmations to change your future.

## CHAPTER NINE NOTES

# CHAPTER TEN

# Your Future is a Thought Away

MANY OF YOU CONTINUALLY think and talk about what you do not want to experience in your life. You forget that the subconscious is a silent listener and it is always turned on and tuned in to you physically, mentally and emotionally. Your subconscious is like having your own personal genie in a lamp. It accepts your thoughts and beliefs as absolute law and seeks to bring them to pass sooner or later. In other words, you think and you get an automatic reaction from your subconscious as the consequence for what you are thinking.

If your conscious mind is full of worry and doubt, your subconscious will take this as an order and give you plenty more to worry about. The conscious mind is responsible for making decisions, choices, and selections. If the conscious mind sends false information to the subconscious, it will use it to produce your request nonetheless. The majority of your negative physical experiences are messages from your subconscious that something is wrong in your belief system.

Your beliefs are the personal laws that you live by. You make choices based on your beliefs. When you believe that you cannot control your physical circumstances, you blame fate or other outside forces for your life experiences. In turn, your emotions expressed in the form of anger, frustration, and resentments create more physical problems in your outside world. If you are not connecting your daily experiences with your thinking, your personal history will continue to repeat itself.

## Christine Changes Her Point of View

Your mental world is your consciousness, and your physical world is the reality of your thoughts and choices. The things you dwell on form mental pictures in your subconscious that will eventually manifest in your body or life experiences.

Christine, a very anxious woman, came to see me after being fired from four different companies in one year. I asked her if she knew why she was terminated from her previous jobs. She said that she did not know the reason, but she was resigned to her fate. From Christine's point of view, her employers and the universe were picking on her. Her future employment looked hopeless and controlled by outside forces. However, outside forces did not control Christine. Her beliefs were the personal laws of her subconscious. *Christine expected to be fired, so she was fired.*

After discussing her situation in depth, I took a flash forward look into Christine's future. Christine's subconscious would keep on repeating its history of termination no matter where she was employed until she reprogrammed her thinking. I also saw another cause of her problems. Christine was a good worker but a major gossiper. If you wanted to know about any of her co-worker's business, just ask Christine. She needed to stop gossiping. Christine had the need to feel important and valuable, but gossiping produced the opposite effect. Christine had to change her mental habits. When she consciously began to look at the cause of her problems and see why she was fired, she was able to change her thinking by developing a healthier attitude and making other choices.

Christine also found other interesting things to talk about. I suggested that she attend a class on developing her communication skills. I recommended that she study subjects she was interested in to improve and extend her areas of interest. I also had her wear a rubber band around her wrist, which I had her snap as a reminder to resist if the urge to gossip returned.

Christine has been working at her present place of employment for five years now. She is popular because she can speak on several interesting topics. Christine was also promoted to a management position, which satisfied her need to feel important. By changing her thinking, she was able to change her future.

You, too, can change your conditions. Your thoughts and choices take physical forms in your body and life experiences as effects. Most all of your future outer, physical experiences are the result of your present, inner thoughts.

## Something to Think About

Besides keeping the physical body functioning, the subconscious is a storehouse of memory. It records your every thought, every word, every emotion, and every action automatically. The next time you consider gossiping behind someone's back, remember that the individual may not be present, but there are no secrets from your subconscious. It is aware of everything you are saying and is recording the whole conversation. The law of cause and effect will give you back what you are giving.

Negative self-talk is when you feed yourself garbage, but you expect a different outcome than what you put in. What goes into your mind also comes out in your physical experiences as the consequences. To trigger your mind not to gossip, get a small statue of the three monkeys to remind you not to talk gossip, not to listen to gossip, and not to read gossip. Keep it at your desk as a trigger mechanism to remind you not to practice negative self-prophecies, gossiping or listening to garbage.

## CHAPTER TEN NOTES

# CHAPTER ELEVEN
# Red Flags Predict the Future

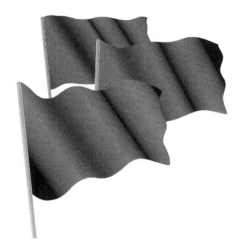

L IFE HAS PERCEIVABLE PATTERNS that can be better understood when you pay attention to existing conditions and experiences. Sometimes a red flag is obvious and direct, but even so there is a tendency to ignore the obvious if you do not want to hear the message. Do not ignore warning signs. What are you presently experiencing? Remember, your physical senses are just as important as your "sixth sense." Your physical senses give you daily information to help you anticipate change and prepare for the future. Carl Jung tells us, "If you are not aware of energy on a conscious level, it manifests on the exterior as fate." If you can see the future in advance, you can intervene to control the outcome. Do not ignore red flags that could save your life.

## Sharon Changes Her Fate
You can learn to detect current circumstances to prepare for the future. Consider the issue of domestic violence. This book is not about domestic violence, but violence in the home between family members, especially adults, is definitely predictable. The following example can be expanded to include other destructive relationships outside of the family circle as well.

Sharon gave up her job as a make-up artist twelve years ago to become a full-time stay-at-home mom. Everything was fine until her husband,

Bill, began coming home late. He had whiskey on his breath and telltale lipstick marks on his shirt collar. Bill would give no excuses for his offensive behavior, and he constantly picked arguments with Sharon. When his cell phone rang, he would move to another room to take the call. Soon he began staying out overnight.

When Sharon asked her husband what was wrong, Bill literally threw a book at her and then beat her up for questioning him. This was the second physical domestic abuse red flag within four months.

When Sharon originally booked a session with me, she hid her black eye behind dark sunglasses and heavy makeup that fooled no one but herself. Sharon was anxious, desperate, and depressed. She was having a difficult time sleeping. She was also angry and resentful. All of these gut feelings were warnings from her subconscious. Sharon did not connect her feelings or her beatings to the red flag warnings. Sharon did not get it! Sharon told me that Bill was not himself and she was waiting for him to change. Say what? Waiting for someone else to change?

I had heard enough. The red flags were all over the place and time was of the essence. Sharon had to change her thinking immediately. Waiting for someone else to change is the biggest cause of loss of control over one's destiny.

I had Sharon relax and flash forward into the future to look at its probabilities if she did nothing to change it today. Sharon refused to recognize the red flags of the predictable future that were everywhere because of her procrastination and wishful thinking. Yet, if nothing changed and things continued the way they were, more serious problems would be the likely outcome. It was obvious to me that she needed to disconnect from Bill physically and leave him immediately. I also suggested getting immediate domestic violence help and joining a group support community.

Sharon continued to ignore the signs. Bill promised that he would change, and he did, for two days, that is. Then the past became the future again. Sharon's next warning was much more dire. Bill was tired of warning Sharon not to ask questions, so he gave her a black eye and a severe punch in the stomach. The black eye was a physical sign to keep Sharon "blind" from seeing the truth about his abuse, while the punch in her solar plexus was to keep her off balance, confused, and controlled by him. This time he also tried to strangle her to make his point: "Shut up, or else!"

Every time Bill physically, mentally, and emotionally abused Sharon, he would try to make her feel guilty and at fault. With a fake tear in his eye, he would control her with a guilt trip. Every time Bill beat up Sharon, he would tell her, "Do you see what you made me do? How can you say you love me when you put me in jail?" Domestic bullies always blame others for their violent behavior. They maintain control by intimidation and justifying their actions with excuses, denials, and declaration of innocence. Do not allow domestic bullies to continue their violence behind closed doors.

Despite Sharon's initial reluctance to take my advice, she eventually accepted my guidance and was prepared, to some extent, when Bill seriously beat her up one more time before leaving her for another woman.

In a follow-up phone call to me, Sharon told me that that Bill was still drinking and had been recently arrested for driving drunk. Sharon felt sorry for Bill, so she borrowed money from a friend and bailed him out of jail. Bill said thanks and then he went back to live with his new girlfriend. Bill seldom saw the children and never phoned them.

Sharon had to take steps to prepare for the future without delay. I suggested that she continue with her domestic violence support group. I also advised her to take professional classes to meet today's demands and brush up on whatever other training she needed to reenter the work environment. Bill continued to drop by to needle Sharon and demanded a divorce within another month. He became so obnoxious that Sharon and the children moved in with her sister until they could afford their own apartment. Sharon began working soon after moving.

Sharon wanted to cut down on expenses by discontinuing her husband's life insurance policy. However, due to her circumstances and a very strong hunch, I advised her to keep up with the payments. If Bill continued his destructive behavior, the outcome was predictable. Eventually, disaster would strike, and it did. Before the divorce was final, a drunk driver killed Bill instantly. I believe that Bill felt guilty and hated himself because of his negative choices and his inability to control himself. Bill's passing was the result of his self-destructive self- programming on a subconscious level.

Bill was dead, but his life insurance policy provided the financial security that the family needed to start all over. If Sharon had not prepared for major life changes, her situation would have been devastating. As you can see, Sharon was in denial. She had to move beyond her fears and let go of her dependency on someone else to make her whole. By taking a flash forward look into her future, she was able to prepare for the outcome while she still had some control.

Although Bill was deceased, he and Sharon were still connected on mental and emotional levels. Most people dwell on the resentments of old heartaches. If you are to let go in your mind, you must consciously apply forgiveness and compassion in your heart. You must learn to release any grudges held from the past. The heart remembers all past pain, but it does not know how to release it. Forgiveness must come from both the conscious and subconscious because, when they unite toward one goal, they heal with compassion and unconditional love. To let go physically, you must first release mentally and emotionally.

## Things to Think About

Violence in domestic and other personal relationships is much more common than most people realize, and it can happen to you. Do not allow bullies to push you around mentally, physically and emotionally. Look at your daily experiences with your partner or other relationships to recognize what you can expect more of in the future. The past is a good indicator of the future in all of your relationships. This includes your family, friends, enemies, and lovers.

Negative patterns are created from your inability to connect the future to your habitual past choices. Albert Einstein tells us, "Insanity is doing the same thing over and over again and expecting different results." The past can show you what you are now avoiding or failing to see today. There is a consequence for all of your choices just as there are physical consequences if you fail to follow traffic laws.

Recognize early red flag warnings before it is too late. Look for early indications that someone may be abusive or insensitive. In the beginning of a relationship there are usually warning signals that you cannot miss if you are paying attention to obvious signals. You may initially mistake possessiveness and jeolousy for caring, but as time passes your abusers attempt to control you will become more evident. Be aware of name calling, accusations, constant criticizing, interrogations, isolation, cruelty, threats, and stalking.

Do not ignore a shove, a slap, a punch in the face, or threats of future violence. Threats are thoughts that may cause physical effects such as beatings or even death in the future. Pay attention to red flags today. Do not make excuses for an abuser. No, you did not have it coming, no matter how many phony excuses are given by the perpetrator to make you feel guilty and keep you silent and afraid. Join a domestic violence support group, read about it, and talk about it to your family and friends. You are not alone. Take action while you still can.

The domestic abuser will intimidate you by trying to separate you from your family and friends. This is an attempt to control you and eliminate all of your physical and emotional support. Like the coward that the bully is, he/she wears many artificial masks and can hide behind scripture, religion, flowers, promises, or outright lies. After all, the goal of the domestic bully is to keep the truth hidden from public or family awareness. Do not let the big smile, huge hug, or phony handshake fool you. The physical abuser is incapable of surviving without you! That is why they consume your energy and leave you drained. All abusers control you by keeping you a prisoner in your own mind. Change your mind by making other choices. Don't be self-victimized by procrastination, your own fears, and psychological blind spots in your thinking.

**Identify Red Flag Warnings**
What are some of the red flags in your life? What can you do today to change the future? Are you prepared to take the necessary physical actions, or are you going to procrastinate until it is too late to change the probable outcome? Use the following flash forward questions to gain a better perspective for understanding the nature of the problem. The solution is sometimes hidden beneath the surface of your subconscious. Use more paper if necessary.

1. Flash forward: Identify the problem in words.
_____
_____
_____
_____

2. Identify the problem emotionally. What are your fears and the
   risk factors?

   _____

   _____

   _____

   _____

3. What is the probable outcome if the problem is not resolved?

   _____

   _____

   _____

   _____

4. What do you feel intuitively?

   _____

   _____

   _____

   _____

5. Initiate a plan of action to change the future.

   _____

   _____

   _____

   _____

## CHAPTER ELEVEN NOTES

# CHAPTER TWELVE

# Childhood Programming

NOW THAT YOU HAVE READ THE BOOK to this point you should have a better understanding of the important role that your subconscious plays in determining future events. An effective way to acknowledge your subconscious is to give it a personal name. The name of my subconscious is Angie. She is my best friend. We are team players as long as we remain on the same page. Get on friendly terms with your subconscious. After all, it has been with you since you were in your mother's womb. Once you give it an identity, talk to it daily as you would a best friend. By establishing a conscious connection with your inner friend, you are improving your communication skills and expanding your world of conscious integration, which includes cooperation, compassion, healing, and intuition.

Your life experiences reveal what your subconscious believes, and this in time becomes your future. Your subconscious has fixed ideas that have been programmed into it since you were a child. Before you had the ability to choose or think for yourself, your parents made your decisions and strongly influenced your thinking. As a result, your self-identification was closely linked with the IDs of your parents. You were skilled according to your parent's point of view, education, and financial status. Consequently, you assumed some of their behavior, attitude, superstitions, fears, opinions, and prejudices.

At the present time, your personality consists of a combination of some of each of your parents' character, plus significant other people that influenced you as a child. You may even have Uncle Henry's red hair, or Grandma Hannah's beautiful blue eyes. Perhaps you inherited your Aunt Millie's creativity to write poems and short stories. Today, you are the sum total of all the people that influenced you as a child, physically, mentally, and emotionally. In turn, you pass down your beliefs, attitudes, likes, and dislikes to your children, who will then pass them down to their own offspring.

Do not blame your parents for your attitude and DNA today. Your mother and father were also programmed by their parents and other significant family members. Today you make decisions based on the past programming of your childhood. Before your reasoning mind could function properly, your subconscious accepted everything you were told as the absolute truth. You may have believed in Santa Claus, the Tooth Fairy, and the Easter Bunny. As you grew older you eventually figured out that these fantasy figures did not exist. You let some of your early childhood beliefs go because you no longer believed in them. However, some of your childhood experiences and programming is still influencing you today even if you may not recall anything in particular. The following are examples of how past programming can still be influencing you today, undetected, but creating future experiences that you do not understand.

### Norman Gets a New Dog Pal

As a child, Norman was warned countless times not to feed stray dogs roaming the neighborhood. One day Norman saw a strange brown dog watching him intently from the middle of a country road. Norman's curiosity got the best of him, and he disregarded his mother's warnings. He ran into the house to get left-over cornbread from the kitchen. Norman lured the dog to come closer to him by throwing small bites of the bread nearer to where he sat on a makeshift wall. Norman should have read the dog's growls, teeth bearing, and barks communicating to him that it did not want to be touched.

Norman began to perspire and feel dizzy. His gut-level feelings were warning him to back off, big time. Instead, Norman ignored the warnings, and the hungry dog came closer. Soon Norman was able to stretch his leg over the crude enclosure to touch the dog on its nose with his bare foot. Norman was immediately bitten several times on his foot and ankle. Oh, what big teeth the dog sank into Norman's flesh! A family member came to his rescue, but not before Norman was badly bitten. The wounds were deep and required several stitches.

Unsurprisingly, Norman avoided all dogs in the future. Norman's subconscious had immediately recorded the painful incident and programmed him to see all dogs as possible threats. His subconscious connected the image of touching the dog to intense physical pain. The apprehension he experienced around dogs was really a gut warning from his subconscious to be careful of all dogs or he could be bitten again. Norman's fear of dogs influenced his behavior for several years even though the incident happened many decades ago. Once Norman was able to identify the cause of his fear of dogs, he was able to instruct his subconscious to release the fear, and it did. Norman is now the proud owner of an older terrier dog, named Bingo. He adopted the dog from the Humane Society. Bingo is loyal, loving, and a great companion to Norman.

## Darlene Learns to Reprogram

Your attitude today depends on your emotional nature. You may be forty-eight years old, but no matter how mature you appear to be today, within you may be a demanding child with a very emotional nature. Your subconscious can approve or disapprove of your conduct and attitude today while influencing your future choices and behaviors.

When Darlene first phoned me for an appointment she insisted that she wanted me to see her right then and there. I could not see her immediately. The harder she tried to intimidate me into seeing her, the more firmly I said no. However, I am a reasonable woman so I scheduled her for a 5:00 p.m. appointment for the next day. I told Darlene to be on time, please. After all, I have my own control issues! The following day she appeared at my door thirty minutes ahead of time. However, I had a phone client, so she had to wait until I completed my other session. I told Darlene to kick back and chill out. At exactly 5:00 p.m., I welcomed her into my home office. I could feel the frost from her body language, but she managed a smile, and, for a moment, the sun came out.

Darlene told me that she had been a sickly child and was very spoiled in her childhood. She received a lot of attention from her parents, uncles, and aunts. Darlene loved attention, but she became temperamental if she felt she was being ignored. Darlene grew older, but she did not outgrow her tantrums.

Despite being forty-eight, Darlene was still having temper tantrums. When she did not get her way, she resorted to anger, tears, name-calling, yelling, and, finally, throwing things. This side of her personality was never revealed to the public. Family members and a few close friends were aware of her moods and behavior. One by one, friends stopped talking to her or had other plans when she inquired about getting together. Darling Darlene was generous, but the friends that remained were the greedy takers. Her phony friends took and took, and temperamental Darlene gave and gave. Insults were sandwiched between acts of kindness and bullying.

After contemplating her story, I decided to flash forward into her future. I closed my eyes and immediately connected to her childhood. It was obvious that if Darlene did not connect her childhood programming to her adult problems they would continue to have power over her. Darlene was using her temper tantrums to control others and to get her way. I told her that her subconscious was in control and her childhood behavior would continue to control her until she consciously changed her attitude. Darlene had to assume responsibility for her choices to change her outer experiences.

The same advice that works for finding misplaced keys could also work for Darlene. I told Darlene that every time she had the urge to lose control, she should backtrack her thinking to reveal the cause of her anger before she acted out emotionally. She should then make a conscious choice to let go of her old programming. She had the power to change her thinking and communicate as an adult. It took a while, but eventually she was able to take control of her life by controlling her thinking, which ruled her emotions.

Take time to review your childhood. Can you recall any prior events that may be influencing you today? What about family members and close childhood friends? Can they recall an incident in your childhood that you may have forgotten?

## Your Subconscious is Predictable

Your future is foreseeable because your subconscious is predictable. It obeys you and responds automatically to your thoughts. You think certain things and you get an automatic reaction from your subconscious according to what you are thinking. The subconscious reacts to the nature of your thoughts. If your mind is full of love, happiness, healing, and other blessed thoughts, you subconscious will respond accordingly. If your subconscious is full of fear, resentment, confusion, and uncertainty it will act in response to these thoughts. Remember, your subconscious accepts everything the conscious mind tells it as the absolute truth and then makes it happen.

The conscious mind is responsible for making right decisions and selections. The subconscious depends on the conscious mind for correct information. If the conscious mind sends false information to the subconscious, it will produce your request nonetheless. It never argues with you or tells you that you are making a mistake. Its business is to work with your conscious mind and produce what you require from the information that you are giving it. The subconscious not only accepts all information as true but acts on it also.

## Lily-Therese Learns a Lesson

The following is an example of how my subconscious responded to my plea for help! As a child I lived in rural Louisiana and was surrounded by nature. My parents always warned me to be on the lookout for poisonous moccasin snakes. One day while walking on a dirt path, I saw a large snake hanging from a moss-covered oak tree limb. I froze in my tracks and was unable to move. My heart began to beat faster, I became nauseous, and I began to sweat profusely as my subconscious prepared me for fight or flight. I decided to run to my home despite the snake's intimidation of me.

As I sprinted past the snake I looked up only to discover that what I thought was a snake was only a long, thick rope. The movement of the draped Spanish moss on the tree limb gave the hanging rope the appearance of a live snake. I sent the mental image of a snake to my subconscious, and it responded automatically to my terror by preparing my body for flight or fight. The subconscious cannot distinguish between fact and fiction, so it had no way of knowing that I sent the wrong information to it. It responded instantly by triggering a gut feeling warning to my physical body. Our feelings are the language of the subconscious.

When I returned home, I tried to explain to my mother why I was late coming home from my grandmother's house. I received a spanking nonetheless because my mother explained that if I had arrived home before sunset, I would not have made the mistake. From that day forward, I always returned home well before dusk. However, despite my caution, I was always uneasy when I approached that particular area. Even though my conscious mind now knew that my prior encounter was not with a real snake, I had developed a fear of snakes. I was programmed. I had developed a fear of the location itself.

It was not until I became an adult that I realized my subconscious had recorded the prior snake occurrence as *real*, and my fear of all snakes was due to that one incident. I eventually remembered that my subconscious is the storehouse of my memory and its job is to recall certain information to save my life. My uneasiness around all snakes was actually a gut feeling warning from my subconscious to help me recall my earlier experiences so that the previous incident would not repeat itself. My conscious mind had to intervene or my subconscious would continue to warn me about all snakes real or imagined in the future. It took many years before I could walk under certain trees without looking up for "snakes," but eventually I was successful.

## Catherine Stops Her Self-Sabotage

Catherine came to see me initially because of a history of failed relationships that began in grammar school. Catherine was attractive and believed that most of her girlfriends were jealous of her, so her circle of friends became smaller and smaller. She told me that all of her previous romantic affairs had failed. As soon as she started dating she would insist that her boyfriends compare her to other attractive women. Heaven help the man that dared to share his honest opinion.

After talking with Catherine for a few minutes, I found out that her father had left her mother, Margaret, for her best friend. As a result, Margaret believed that all men and women should not be trusted. Margaret unknowingly passed on her distrust in relationships to her daughter, Catherine. Past programming now ruled her behavior and sabotaged all of her relationships. Catherine had to release her negative programming or the future would continue to repeat the past. This lady now expected all of her relationships to fail, and they did. To change her outer experiences, she had to make the changes in her mind first. Catherine forgave herself for her incorrect thinking and began to affirm that the right man for her was in her life now. Happiness and love were her divine rights, and she gave thanks daily for her successful relationships. Time was passing, but thank God her biological clock was still ticking. After about eight months, Catherine phoned to update me with some great news. Catherine told me that she was getting married to one of her former boyfriends. Of course, I was invited to the wedding.

## Hypnosis and the Power of Suggestion

Your future can be influenced by the power of suggestions other than those from your subconscious. Your daily thinking can be controlled, motivated, inspired, and changed by persuasion, meditation, affirmations, commands, implication, and the power of hypnosis. The subconscious can be tricked by hypnosis to produce certain effects. Whatever your subconscious accepts as facts it produces in your physical world as effects. Hypnosis is an artificially induced condition that reveals how suggestions made to the subconscious can modify one's perception of reality and experience.

Hypnosis demonstrates how receptive the subconscious is to the power of suggestion, even if it is tricked into believing a lie. For example, a professional hypnotist may suggest to an individual that he is a famous actor, and the subject will begin to act the part without an acting lesson. The mental suggestion that you are a great rock star will reveal rock 'n roll talent that you did not show previously. The suggestion to your subconscious that an object will burn you upon contact will produce a physical burn even if it is as cold as an ice cube.

If you question the power of suggestion, all you need do is listen to the radio or watch TV to hear how commercials influence the consumer to purchase products. You are conditioned to respond automatically to advertisements with verbal and visual triggers. Commercials use beautiful men and women to sell their products, which imply that if you purchase what they are selling you too can have the good life and even look like the perfect models. Imagine you are watching television when a food commercial comes on. You look hungrily at a large hamburger and fries even though you ate dinner only two hours earlier. Certain words, gestures, and imagery are programming you to respond in certain ways.

Successful advertising campaigns appeal to your emotional needs, goals, dreams, and fears. Repeated suggestions act through your physical senses, overcoming logic and reason. The power of suggestion acts directly on your feelings and emotions. If you do not connect your thinking to your feeling, you will be out the door in a matter of minutes to buy the extra-large hamburger combo. If your automatic response to food commercials continues, you can predict that you will be overweight in a matter of weeks. Very few things are controlled by destiny. Therefore, most of the future is subject to change and modification. The subconscious is very open to the power of suggestion and can easily be influenced by your own conscious mind as well. Hypnosis is also used to effectively treat some phobias, improve study habits, quit bad habits, lose weight and reduce stress. A number of studies have shown that hypnotherapy can be used to ease the pain of childbirth and treat headaches and chronic pain without drugs or side effects.

**Things to Think About**

The past can create future problems out of habit. Can you can see how the child controls you in the present day, influencing you to do what it wants to do according to your past programming. In fact, your subconscious is the judge and the jury that determines all of your future experiences according to how you are programmed. All negative beliefs, fears, disapprovals, and personality traits are passed down to future generations. These negative mental suggestions take seed in the soil of the child's subconscious and begin to take physical forms in their experiences later as adults. Today, your subconscious beliefs direct your perception of the way you see the world even if you live to be one hundred years old. Your physical body and mind are connected so your mental state determines all of your outside physical experiences automatically.

Your subconscious retains memories as pictures in mental forms. Your thoughts are mental photographs in your mind, which produce your outer physical conditions as effects. When the conscious mind thinks of an image, the subconscious has to produce the exact physical form in your outside world. If you hold an image of what you do not want, the subconscious will still produce the exact physical form anyway because it cannot choose or reason on its own.

# CHAPTER TWELVE NOTES

CHAPTER THIRTEEN

# Fragrances Link Us to Memories

D O YOU KNOW THAT some of your future life experiences are associated with particular scents that are recognized deeply in your
subconscious? Smells, moods, and memories are all linked as one shared
experience. Aromatherapy practices the healing power of essential oils to
enhance psychological and physical well-being. Smells also act as triggers to
help you recall good or bad experiences. Scents can influence your future
behavior when they are associated with a particular event or experience.
The scent of a particular flower smelled at a loved one's memorial service
will trigger an emotional response today even if it took place decades ago.

Various scents activate centers in the body and mind, stimulating them
into action to influence your moods and behaviors. Scents link you to memories that convey special meaning and communicate what words alone cannot do to touch you through your feelings. The following are examples of
how certain scents can influence your behavior and create future experiences.

## Katherine Needs More Sense than Scents

Katherine was a twenty-eight-year-old Southern belle, born and raised in
Georgia. She loved the beautiful magnolia tree that thrived in her next-

door neighbor's back yard. The scent of its beautiful flowers was her favorite fragrance. Until she met Andy, that is. Katherine fell head over heels in love with the man, and he soon moved in with her despite the fact that she had known him only a short time. Andy had strong opinions, and he soon influenced Katherine's choices in every area of her life. Andy did not like the smell of magnolias because he said it reminded him of his former girlfriend. Katherine wanted Andy to forget the past, so she changed her own fragrance fast. However, the new scent reminded him of his ex-wife, so she stopped using Chanel #5. Next she tried fragrances from Christian Dior and Estee Lauder, but they also reminded him of other women. Finally, out of desperation, she stopped using perfume altogether.

Unfortunately for Katherine, it turned out that Andy had strong opinions about clothing as well. No matter what she wore, it always reminded him of someone else. It was an intensive, passionate relationship while it lasted, but the fire burned out fast. When she was able to finally see through the ashes, Katherine got the message and kicked Andy to the curb.

What Katherine needed to begin with was more sense, not scents. Katherine is back to wearing the magnolia fragrance because she loves it. In the future, she is not going to make any exceptions regarding her choices in anything else to please a man. Of course, if she is unwilling to make some changes, she may be better off without a man at all than with one that wants to change her.

## Anna Changes an Outcome

Some scents can recall unpleasant experiences and affect you when you least expect it. Anna lost control at a friend's home when watermelon slices were served at lunchtime. Watermelon trigged the recollection of the death of her mother two years earlier. Anna's mother was canning watermelon preserves when she died suddenly of a heart attack in the presence of her daughter. From that time forward Anna's subconscious recalled the tragic image of her mother's death by linking it to the aroma of watermelon.

The solution was to let go of the unpleasant memory and replace it with a positive experience. She could get help in doing this by looking at old photos of herself and her mother in happier times. Anna could choose a photo that appealed to her and use it as a new line of code to reprogram her subconscious to remember the good times they spent together. This simply required reprogramming her emotional response by changing her thinking. Anna also made a deliberate decision to choose the fragrance of roses to redirect her subconscious when she thinks of her mother. Scents do, indeed, influence your moods and behavior.

## Lily-Therese and Gingerbread Memories

I have a pleasant memory triggered by the smell of ginger. I remember helping my mother bake gingerbread men when I was a child. I recall the wonderful scent of ginger and other captivating kitchen spices. I can recall my mother patting me on my head and telling me how helpful I was to the family. Today, the smell of ginger acts as a positive trigger and takes me right back to the age of six, making me feel happy, loved, and proud. In fact, just looking at a box of ginger snaps in the grocery store makes the connection. The smell of ginger links me to a living memory of my mother and a positive experience today even though she died over twenty-five years ago. Happy memories trigger happy future recollections, so I use this technique consciously to influence my subconscious and enhance my life.

## CHAPTER THIRTEEN NOTES

# CHAPTER FOURTEEN
# Your Feelings Create your Future

W E RESPOND TO LIFE on an automatic, emotional level. *Your emotions are your body's response to mental images created when you think about the world around you.* Most people believe that they are not responsible for their feelings. However, you are responsible for how you feel. *What you think about creates how you feel, and how you feel creates your behavior.* You cannot have a feeling without having a thought first. If you are sad or angry, you first have to have thoughts that made you feel sad or angry.

When you find yourself depressed or out of control, review the thoughts that preceded your feelings. Become aware of how many times a day you lose control because of your emotions. You react to life because of your past programming. When you believe yourself to be in a stressful situation, your defense mechanism automatically turns on, giving you the extra adrenaline for fight-or-flight. Of course, the size of your opponent may be a deciding factor.

Overreacting to daily problems as though they were life-threatening experiences will keep your body in a constant state of fight or flight. When anger, hatred, resentment and other emotions form a chain reaction, the subconscious has no means of knowing that you are not in an actual fight-or-flight emergency. For example, if a car cuts you off on the highway and you respond by getting angry, cussing the driver, and giving him the middle finger, your subconscious will automatically pump up your adrenaline to prepare you for fight or flight.

Sometimes the other person will respond by turning your actions back on you like a boomerang. Rage intimidates and sometimes kills. Adrenaline is an extremely powerful hormone produced in high-stress situations.

Too much adrenaline can cause serious problems when it is not released. Your thoughts influence your behavior and moods. The following example will offer you another perception of looking at things that you may never have considered before reading this.

## Jimmy Jumps to Conclusions

Joan and Jimmy were having a great day at the beach with their friends. They were invited to a party later that evening. Joan's ex-boyfriend also happened to be there. Although the ex-couple avoided each other completely, Jimmy soon began to get angry, thinking that they were giving each other the eye behind his back. Jimmy invited Harry to step outside to talk about the situation, but Harry was not a talker. Joan had neglected to tell Jimmy that her ex-boyfriend was a professional boxer. Their "conversation" did not last long before Jimmy was down for the count.

The evening went downhill after that. After Jimmy regained consciousness, he demanded that they leave the party immediately. Jimmy accused Joan of flirting with her old beaux, and Joan accusing him of being jealous and throwing the first punch. This is the perfect example of how your emotions take away your power to see things clearly. Nothing whatsoever was going on behind Jimmy's back. Every emotion that Jimmy experienced was preceded by a suspicious thought, which took him away from reason and logic. Jimmy's thinking was then the cause of the breakup of the two-year relationship. If he does not make changes in his thinking, his future relationships will end because of his jealousy issues.

## Marie's Thoughts are Linked to Her Emotions

Our emotions follow our thoughts and can change our mood in moments. For example, Marie woke up in a great mood. The day before, she had received a big promotion and a salary increase of $5,000 a year. She was thinking of what she would purchase with the extra money when the telephone rang. It was a call from her mother to let her know that her brother had been seriously injured in a motorcycle accident. Marie began crying immediately even though only a few moments earlier she had been very happy. You may not understand that your feelings are connected to your thoughts and are the physical reactions to your thinking. You cannot experience an emotion without experiencing a physical change as well. Before the phone call, Marie was feeling wonderful. It is only after she heard of her brother's accident that she became extremely depressed.

## Your Subconscious Responds to your Emotions

The subconscious depends on the conscious mind for its orders and directions. As I have said previously, if you give it false information or the wrong images, it will respond automatically nonetheless. It accepts what you say or think literally and delivers what you ask for as soon as possible. It cannot take a joke, but it can create your future experiences. The conscious mind must give the order to let go to the subconscious before it can do so. The subconscious responds automatically to what the conscious mind is picturing. It can only receive or accept your orders. It cannot let go on its own because it depends on the conscious mind for its instructions.

If your subconscious is loaded with fears and doubts, you will be unable to let them go without the intervention of your conscious mind. There *must* be no conflict between the conscious and subconscious or you will get what you have mentally accepted. There must be cooperation between the conscious and subconscious toward the same goal. You cannot have opposing beliefs if you want to move forward.

For example, if you want to experience a loving relationship on a conscious level but think you do not deserve it on a subconscious level; you will not experience a loving relationship. Your subconscious accepts your thoughts and beliefs as absolute laws and then brings them to pass. Whatever thoughts you accept in your mind, you also accept in your physical body and affairs.

## Daniel Stops Sabotaging Himself

Most people do not know that their conscious mind may believe in one thing but the subconscious may believe in something else entirely. For example, you may have a conscious desire to make a lot of money, but if your subconscious believes that money is the root of all evil, you will never be able to bring your full abilities to making money. Holding two conflicting thoughts in your mind at the same time is known in psychology as cognitive dissonance.

For example, Daniel initially came to me complaining of his lack of money. He was agitated, angry, jealous, and resentful of prosperous people. I took a flash forward look into his future and discovered that his problems were the result of a conflict between the conscious and subconscious. Daniel had two opposing beliefs. On a conscious level, Daniel desired to be prosperous, but he resented prosperous people on a subconscious level. Indeed, he called successful people only "folks with good luck." He also believed that money was the root of all evil. Therefore, his subconscious gave him what it thought he wanted: nothing.

I had to help Daniel redirect his subconscious, or he would never develop a prosperity consciousness. The solution was to let go of his bitterness and resentment regarding money. Daniel had to be thankful when his friends achieved a raise or promotion.

If you want to be blessed and successful, do not resent blessed and successful people. How do you react when someone around you has some good things happen? Do you congratulate them, or do you get angry and resentful? Being jealous of other people's blessings can interfere with the flow of your own miracles in the making. You must learn to bless persons, places, and things in your daily life because everything you have or do not have is your expression of the universal law of cause and effect.

Daniel needed to reprogram his subconscious or he was doomed to be bitter and broke. Once Daniel changed his attitude, he was able to let go of the negative mental conditions that kept him angry and poor.

Daniel gave me a phone call update six months later with great news. He told me that about one month after his visit with me his luck began to change. He had won a small amount of money from a lottery and he was thankful for the gift. He could hardly wait to tell me his more recent great news. Three months ago his company expanded to include locations overseas. His employer now offered perks to employees willing to relocate to overseas assignments. Daniel decided that he was flexible enough to proceed with the necessary training that his new position required.

Upon the completion of his training he was promoted, given an expense account, and a ticket across the seas. As long as Daniel uses good judgment he has employment security, and cultural diversity. Daniel said, yes, yes, yes to prosperity, and the universe begin to give, give, and give! Daniel thanked me over and over and wished me good luck.

I accepted his blessings. The next day I was looking for a business card and found a $100 bill I had placed several years back in a book, *The Dynamic Laws of Prosperity*, by Catherine Ponder. Open the doors to your own treasure chest of prosperity and potential. Your subconscious is the treasure chest, and your conscious mind is the key that unlocks it.

**Things to Think About**

Your conscious mind must give the "let go" order to the subconscious. Daniel had to forgive himself and let go of the people he resented on a conscious level before his subconscious could also let go of resentment. Forgiveness and letting go are constant processes. Your conscious mind can delete undesirable data in the subconscious and replace it with constructive information. The conscious mind can delete old cycles and reprogram the subconscious to change your future. You cannot experience anything new if you hold on to your old attitudes of anger, hate, jealousy, grudge holding and resentment. To complete all cycles, you must let go mentally before you can begin to receive physically.

CHAPTER FOURTEEN NOTES

# CHAPTER FIFTEEN

# Omens and Grandmother's Wisdom

Roots, illustration by Liz-Ann Konn

OMENS WERE TAKEN VERY SERIOUSLY by our early ancestors, who were strongly connected to their roots in nature. They looked to omens for guidance in relationships, healing, productivity, fertility, survival, hunting/gathering, decision-making, and meaning in their day-to-day lives. When people were few and lived far apart from each other, their neighbors included the wild animals who taught them how to survive. The significance of dreams, omens, and signs were instinctively understood.

Ancient people trusted their omens and feelings to sense unseen dangers and impending disasters all around them. The Creator talked to them through their intuition and physical senses. Passing clouds in the heavens, a flight of birds in the air, an energetic, fast-moving wild animal, a breath-taking rainbow, a flash of lightning in the skies, and the howl of a coyote were all-important omens and messages from the realm of Spirit.

Although, we are surrounded in an all-knowing spiritual presence of intelligence that has the answers to all of our needs we sometimes ignore the voice of Spirit. Everyday ordinary people receive countless messages about the future, but they don't register in the conscious mind because we are too distracted to pay attention. To the sophisticated person of today, seeking messages and omens from nature may appear to be an outdated and superstitious form of communication. However, even now it is foolish to dismiss omens because they are linked to our subconscious from birth. Today, omens remain an influential source of information regarding our daily living and future. Observing signs and omens can be a powerful source of insight, protection, instruction, and guidance. It is up to each one of us to understand their meaning and apply the wisdom in our daily living. Omens can be good or bad, depending on different people's interpretation of them.

Learning to interpret omens can reveal coming events if you pay attention. What is the message of the white cloud in the sky shaped like a bridge? What about lightning that struck close to the tree next to you? What was the omen of seeing a horned owl in the daytime? What about finding the rock that is shaped like a heart? What about the tree that has naturally formed faces on its trunk?

Some omens are obvious when interpreted according to your current issues. Knowing what lies ahead can prevent serious penalties in your everyday world. When you fail to read your environment, the consequence may be accidents, mistakes, or even death. Each of you has the ability to interpret an omen if you pay attention to what nature is trying to tell you. If you do not like the probable outcome, you can intervene to change the future.

Nature can be a profoundly beneficial source of experience when you pay attention with all of your physical senses. Mother Earth has a voice in what you hear, see, and feel. In your modern urban lives, the subtle sounds of nature are silenced by loud, modern distractions. It is unsurprising that you feel detached from your environment. There are natural healing benefits when you sleep under the shining stars at night, walk alongside tall trees in the daytime, explore hidden valleys in autumn, and listen to the sound of ocean waves and swiftly running streams in the summertime. Take time to listen to the sounds of birds singing on a cool autumn morning. Silently watch a bubbling creek tumble and fall over rocks and stones. Observe a deer leap gracefully through the air effortlessly. Become the deer in your imagination. What does it feel like to be wild, free, and strong? Feel the energy of the revitalizing sun as it heals you and connects you to the element of fire.

Today, with every technological "miracle," you grow further apart and more disconnected from your ancient roots. It is difficult to keep connected to nature when your only activity is limited to the technology of text messaging, surfing the Internet, playing video games, and chatting on social media. If you do not pay attention to what you are doing, distractions in your physical world can make you an accident waiting to happen. The benefit of having a cell phone is great, but for the person distracted while talking or texting, it could mean death or an accident. For example, a woman recently shot to fame when she fell into a Dallas mall water fountain while completely distracted by texting on her cell phone.

Remember that your thoughts control your behavior and feelings. If you argue on your cell phone and your emotions disconnect you from paying attention to the physical world, you will experience a mental and bodily disconnection as well. Feeling spaced out is a mental disconnection. Technology can disconnect you from your intuitive sense and blind you to seeing omens. Omens usually have to shout loudly at you to catch your attention. Every day, motorists are bombarded with visual advertising images selling everything you can possibly think of. Advertisements for video games, movies, TV shows, mobile phones, men's clubs, women's spas, political campaigns, food, drinks, and credit cards dare us to ignore them. Vivid colors, dramatic eye-grabbing pictures, and witty slogans command our attention, and all this is very distracting.

Other physical symbols direct, warn, inform, and protect us from physical dangers in our material world. Traffic signs are an example of a critical element in the safe and efficient control of our environment. Traffic signs warn us of potential hazards. When we pay attention and obey traffic signs, we avoid problems, accidents, and possibly death. Omens also offer us the same guidance and protection in our personal lives. Omens are like blinking, eye-catching, energy signals. They are beneficial to us only when we notice them and act on their messages.

Today, nature's omens and intuition are still a natural, important part of your heritage, but they can be locked out by a mind obsessed with facts, figures, uncertainty, fear, and worry. Cultivating a relationship with nature will definitely help you see omens and signs when you look for them. To increase your sensitivity and awareness in nature, spend time in the great outdoors. Sleep under the stars, or try gardening, bird watching, camping, backpacking, walking, boating, fishing, and getting acquainted with the wildlife in your environment. Go to the zoo, listen, and observe omens all around you.

## Grandmother Interprets Omens

My profession as a holistic intuitive specialist was highly influenced by my childhood teachings from my grandmother. Grandmother was a wise, intuitive, practical, and no nonsense woman. Grandmother believed that lessons from nature's omens could provide people with significant insight into coming times. She believed that we were connected to everything in our environment. If folks paid attention to existing conditions and experiences, they could predict future occurrences. Some people sought her advice, intuitive skills, and home remedies on a regular basis. Grandmother was always available with the appropriate herbal medicines, prayers, and talismans. If someone had troubles, Grandmother had the solutions. Grandmother was never paid money for her services. Instead she received gifts such as eggs, vegetables, chickens, rice, pecans, seasonal fruits, jars of homemade preserves, honey, cakes, and home-baked bread.

Grandmother firmly believed that something had to be given in exchange for her services. She was willing to barter as an exchange of energy. Small problems usually required weeding her garden, getting wood for her stove, or running errands. Bigger problems were paid for with more physical work. Grandmother told me that physical labor helped take the people's minds off of their troubles by putting their energy into something more constructive. Grandmother strongly believed that people could think themselves sick. She was quick to point out how effective her treatments were. Why, just hearing the physical labor that Grandmother required of them to resolve their problems miraculously cured many people without her doing anything.

Although I lived at home with my parents and siblings, I spent a lot of time with my grandparents. Grandmother showed me my deep roots in nature. She really knew how to read omens, and she was nearly always right about what to expect in the future. She told me that the trick to reading omens was to keep in rhythm with nature by paying attention to the environment.

Speaking of omens, I was born at home with a veil or membrane covering my face. The caul was considered an omen of second sight. On the day of my birth, a white dove flew into the house and landed on my cradle. To Grandmother this was another positive omen that I was linked to the dove or the Holy Spirit. The dove is the symbol of the messenger, peace, hope, guidance, love, and prophecy. Grandmother said that I had to live up to the spiritual significance, so she decided to teach me the old ways.

As time passed, I watched and listened to my Grandmother with great interest. Grandmother was convinced that early signs based on information received from the physical senses and intuition were strong indications of what to expect. She told me that the future could always be observed in the present time.

Grandmother paid attention to people's complaints. She observed their body talk in the forms of headaches, backaches, sore throats, indigestion, diarrhea, warts, fevers, and the like. She linked their health issues with bad choices and thoughts that did not agree or digest well with them. Problems were also perceived as being in disagreement with the environment. She could interpret dreams before people finished a first cup of coffee and read them faster than I could pump up a glass of water from the well. I could go on and on, but I think that you get the picture.

One morning, Grandmother woke me up early to give me a lesson from nature. I looked at the clock meaningfully, but Grandmother ignored me. Then I thought of a great idea and told her I had a bellyache. That was my first mistake of the day. She peered into my face, opened an old cupboard, and pulled out a large bottle of homemade herbal medicine. She then got a tablespoon out of a drawer and walked over to my bed. Grandmother said to open my mouth and she would give me a dose of "something" to cure me. I jumped out of bed and told her that it would not be necessary after all because I was already feeling so much better. Grandmother said that her medicine was so powerful that in this case I did not even have to swallow it to get cured. I agreed entirely. After looking at me suspiciously for a few more moments, she returned the bottle to its shelf, and I begin to breathe again.

I reluctantly sat down at the kitchen table and began to eat my breakfast. It was couche couche, a homemade cereal consisting of fried cornmeal, sugar, and canned milk mixed with water. I loved it, but I hesitated to eat too fast and get her thinking I had intestinal worms and giving me a dose of her powerful medicine. Yikes!

I watched Grandmother for clues to her mood, and she watched me for indications of other issues I might not have told her about earlier. After breakfast, Grandmother handed me old, dark blue coveralls and a red plaid flannel shirt with yellow elbow patches.

After dressing, I hurriedly put on a pair of mismatched socks and my old brown high-top leather "working" boots. For the final touch, I covered my head with grandfather's old worn-out straw hat. Unfortunately, the hat keep slipping over my face or falling off of my head. After watching me pick up the hat several times, Grandmother looked me over with one eye and said, "Humbug!" She hurried to her sewing basket and returned with a long black shoelace. She poked two holes in the hat with her scissors and passed the shoelace through the holes. She then tied the hat firmly under my chin and told me to wait for her outside. When Grandmother was out of hearing distance, I whispered, "Humbug."

Grandmother soon joined me outside. She was wearing a faded, long-sleeved, rust-colored shirt, a long brown skirt, a calico apron, and an old pair of black boots and black stockings. She wore an ancient faded sun-bonnet on her head and carried her cane. She handed me a cloth sack in the event that we ran across anything interesting. Despite the cane, she was a fast walker. I slowly followed her down a long, winding dirt path, mumbling and stumbling.

After a few minutes, Grandmother looked back over her shoulder and motioned for me to walk faster. I was sweating by the time that I caught up with her, but I was in a better mood. I was pleased when we finally came to rest near a marshy creek. It was a beautiful sunny day. A slight breeze whispered through moss-draped oak trees, and the environment danced with life. Iridescent dragonflies lighted lazily on the surface of the water. We watched three turtles sunning themselves on an old log in the water. Curious fluttering butterflies and birds of many species flew happily in the air and sang in the trees.

When I received a rap on the foot from my grandmother's cane for apparently the second time, it got my full attention. She told me to listen and observe the environment for omens and signs. She emphasized her point with another rap on my boot. When she turned her head to look at something, I quickly moved further away from her cane. Grandmother told me to watch a mother raccoon moving her babies away from the edge of the water to higher ground. She said that raccoons were active at night, so daytime activity was a sure sign that something was up. In a few minutes Grandmother told me to get up. She said that a bad storm was approaching, and we needed to go home immediately to prepare for it.

The sun was still shining, the sky was still clear, and the birds were still singing. It was difficult to believe that soon we would be hit with the fury of a tropical storm. When we got home, Grandfather was told to cover the windows with wooden boards. I pumped extra water from the well into a large bucket and dragged it slowly inside the small house. We got out extra kerosene for the lamps and brought in more firewood for the cooking stove. The cabin was not wired with electricity, so we did not have to worry about the lights or refrigerator going out. We did not have running water or indoor plumbing, so that took care of a lot of other needless worrying.

After securing the cabin, Grandfather took a nap in an old cast iron bed with a soft, moss-filed mattress and big feather pillows. Soon he was snoring loudly. Grandmother told me to wash up. She did not have to tell me twice! I poured water from an ancient-looking clay pitcher into an old blue enameled washbasin and quickly washed my face and hands. I glanced at Grandmother to see if she had noticed that I had not used the homemade soap she had placed next to the water basin. I did not have to worry because she was preoccupied. I watched her as she added more wood to feed the hungry stove, lit a kerosene lamp, and placed it on top of an old brown highboy in the kitchen area. Within two hours, the energy of the environment began to change. We could feel the electricity in the air, which increased with the coming of the moaning wind.

Although Grandmother's cat, Miss Kitty, was an outdoor cat, she demanded to be let inside the cabin. In another few minutes Grandpa's dog, Peanut, began to howl, but I was told to put him in a small shed in the backyard. I gave Peanut extra food and water. He looked up at me pleadingly with his big brown eyes, but before I closed the shed door he made a mad dash for the food. Outside the activity of the birds and animals grew. I watched as the chickens ran squawking into the hen house and a neighbor's pig tried to join them. An angry rooster with ruffled neck feathers blocked the pig from entering. I had already been attacked by the Boss, as Grandfather referred to the rooster, and I knew that he would not back down if it came to a fight with the pig. The nervous pig sensed it also and ran squealing back into loud roars of thunder. When I returned to the cabin, I think I saw the cat smiling.

Outside, the winds howled and thunder roared. Lightning crackled and the sky grew dark and ominous. Large, gray clouds begin to gather in thick, black clumps. However, the outside weather was nothing compared to the mood that I was in after cleaning up after the cat. Miss Kitty had developed a bad case of diarrhea due to her physical senses that triggered her survival instinct. Instinct had definitely put her in a survival mode, but she was able to let go of some of her fears. I would have liked to hide under the bed, but the cat had already claimed this spot for the duration of the tropical storm.

Grandmother said that what went on outside was not to distract us from our ability to work inside. I asked her about the inside of the cabin because cleaning up after the cat had really distracted me. Grandmother said that I should be grateful that I had physical senses. She said in this particular situation to be especially thankful for my nose, which indicated where I should look before I walked to prevent more problems.

In Grandmother's eyes, we had to take advantage of every opportunity. Being prepared and the ability to adapt to change were vital to survival. Grandmother believed that nature would talk to us to help us to survive if we paid attention with our physical senses and listened with our intuitive heart. She said that if I observed my environment nature would whisper her secrets in the warm summer breezes, in the rustling of the leaves, and in the twinkling stars high in the night skies, and the wild animals would teach me to survive.

Indeed, Grandmother had read the omens from the raccoons correctly. Grandmother told me that animals relied on instinct and paid attention to all information coming through their physical senses. This allows them to react to certain environmental changes faster than human beings do. Animals thus reveal nature's messages.

How do omens talk to you? Do you act on them, or do you ignore them? How have omens helped you in the past?

# CHAPTER FIFTEEN NOTES

# CHAPTER SIXTEEN
# Wild Animals Predict the Future

Snow Leopard, illustration by Vernon O. Wilffong

I F YOU WATCH NATURE, you will receive messages directly from the animals, insects, birds, and plants. A visit from a fox could indicate that it is time to develop your cunning skills before dealing with tricky people or situations. For some cultures the raven and the owl are messengers that indicate bad omens. But the symbolism of these same beautiful birds may be interpreted entirely differently by other groups of people. In fact, the symbolic meanings of animals can differ greatly from person to person. Omens should be interpreted according to your personal circumstances.

Sometimes, animals will not wait for you to go to them to give you their messages. Wild animals will come to you! I have recently experienced receiving messages from coyotes, raccoons, horned owls, hawks, crows, and a fox. They appeared everywhere in my backyard. In the morning, afternoon, and evening, they showed up like unexpected, hungry guests. Wild animals represent the subconscious, through which we are all linked to the world. Since all of nature is connected at an unseen level, seeing the wild animals in the physical world definitely got my attention. By observing nature, I realized the animals lived one day at a time and were willing to change and adapt to circumstances no matter where they existed.

Wild animals represent movement, change, adaptation, survival, and relocation. Nothing distracts them from attaining their objectives, and they are not restricted by the time of day. Fences, gates, locks, and other deterrents do not restrain them because they are born wild and free. They are willing to cross boundaries, walls, and fences to survive.

Could I do the same? I had to step over the self-imposed boundaries of my own thinking, procrastination, and fears to move forward with this book. This was the message of the wild animals to me! The creatures asked me to step out of my comfort zone. The little masked-bandit raccoons wanted me to see beyond the outer mask of my personality and get in touch with my authentic self. The coyotes wanted me to be less serious so I could see past the surface of the obvious and adapt to new situations with laughter. The great horned owls wanted me to focus on my intentions and move swiftly toward my goals. The hawk's message was to look at the bigger picture to soar and glide upon the wings of change. The crow's message was for me to initiate transformation and interpret the mysterious in the seen and unseen worlds. The fox's message was to keep my cloak of invisibility and camouflage ready for when I need my privacy.

You, too, should watch the animals and birds to see how they survive, prepare, and respond to their environment because it is essential to your own survival. The animals, plants, minerals, and insects will talk to you loudly or silently about the future. To communicate, cougars growl, birds sing, owls hoot, bobcats hiss, lions roar, and hawks circle.

Most animals focus on their day-to-day requirements to survive. Animals speak to us through their behavior. Paying attention to the animals as omens will help you prepare for seasonal changes and plan ahead for the future. Animal instinct is the power of knowing something without previous knowledge, memory or experience. Some birds know when to fly south for the winter *before* the weather turns cold, some bears know when to lie dormant before freezing conditions occur, and thrifty squirrels instinctively know when to collect and hide food before it becomes in short supply. The more you focus on your connection to nature, the faster you will receive guidance from everything in your environment. You will begin to observe omens everywhere. Visit a local park, listen, and silently watch for messages from nature.

Observe the animals, birds, and insects in your own backyard. The nature of omens is that they are simple, easy to recognize, and to the point. All animals know how to adapt to survive despite their species. The same Universal Spirit that guides them through instinct also guides you through intuition. The animal's strength and character also reflect human characteristics. Think about the animals that you see in your dreams. Are you attracted to a particular animal? Does a bear or a wolf call out to you? When you visit the zoo, what is the first animal that you look for? Are you a collector of stuffed animals or pictures? Are you attracted to t-shirts that feature specific animals?

Each animal has certain powers to teach and knowledge to share. When a particular animal appears in your life, you can determine what its message is by the nature of the animal and your present circumstances. The nature of omens and intuition may not be fully understood in a technological sense, but each animal has its own method of overcoming the many challenges it has met to survive. Be aware of the repeated appearance of some animals. Open your mind and assume a receptive attitude of trust and faith. Realize that all things are interconnected and you are a vital part of the whole with a telepathic connection to everything. Everything is alive because Spirit is present everywhere. Everything, including the past, is recorded in the energy of Mother Earth.

What is your perception of the animal kingdom? Can you read the body language of a friend and compare it with a wild animal on the prowl? How do your react when you feel threatened or afraid? Do you feel like the prey or the predator in an unfamiliar setting at night? What animals do you identify with in your daytime hours and in your nighttime dreams? The animal kingdom is able to survive because it is guided by instinct. The following are examples of how animals can predict the future.

**Lily-Therese Gets a Message from the Ants**
Some messages from nature are subtle and can easily be missed if you are not paying attention. If ants invade your home, think of the message

before you kill the messengers. When ants enter your life, it is time for you to pay attention and learn something about yourself. For example, several years ago, I experienced a major ant invasion. No matter how hard I tried, I could not get rid of these little insects. Ants were everywhere. Yikes!

Sometimes the same species will appear repeatedly until you get their message. It was obvious that I had to change my perception of the ant invasion in order to get the significance of their message. I thought of the meaning of ants and how I could link their behavior to my situation. All of a sudden I got it! This is what they were communicating to me: "Request help with a project. Become a team player. Do not try to carry a load on your own. Gain the cooperation of other people. There is strength in numbers." I was working on a project that required help, and I was hesitating in asking for assistance. As soon as I requested help, the ant problem went away on its own. At the time, I thought that it was a coincidence.

## The Raccoons Give Lily-Therese a Warning

One night quite a number of years ago, I had a forewarning dream that featured just the head of a raccoon staring at me. The mask around its eyes was really exaggerated. What really got my attention was when its eyeballs literally popped out as in a cartoon. The next morning about 10 a.m. while walking in the hills, I suddenly encountered a frisky raccoon in the daytime, which was strange because raccoons are nocturnal animals. It was trying to steal a half-eaten apple from someone's open lunch box left under a tree. I continued my walk and was surprised to see yet another raccoon in the daylight. This smart raccoon was trying to steal crayfish from an improvised trap. The trapper had used fresh chicken gizzards as bait to lure the crawdads into the snare. From the sounds coming from an ice chest that sat next to the creek, I knew that there was going to be a crawfish boil for dinner.

*Yum, yum,* I thought as I looked around for the trapper. No one was in sight so I continued my walk. Now I really began to pay attention. Counting the larger-than-life mask of the raccoon in my dream, I had seen three raccoons. What was the message?

Sometimes seeing the same species of wild animal will give you a better understanding of the significance of their message if is linked to your present circumstances. I stopped walking and stood still to get in touch with my gut feelings. What were my physical senses telling me about my environment? I closed my eyes to focus on the unseen, which gave me a flash forward look into the future. In my mind's eye, I instantly saw the larger-than-life raccoon mask of my dream, and then I received a vivid image of my car. I made the leap in a mental picture. When I tuned into my gut feelings, my intuition kicked in to give me a complete picture.

The creature's mask was a definite warning of a robbery. I did not need to see another raccoon to get the point. Although I had locked my car before starting my walk, I rushed to where I had parked it. I was just in time to see two young men stealing things from the vehicle parked next to my car. I was unquestionably next on their agenda. The shifty-looking characters were placing items they had stolen in a heap next to their van. I blew loudly on my whistle, which I always wear around my neck when walking. The shrill sound startled the thieves, who immediately jumped into their van without picking up their stolen items. The side panel of the vehicle featured a photo of raccoon. This was definitely a significant message from the raccoon detectives, and I got it!

## Wild Animals Adapt to Survive

Nature does not require wild animals to act on reason to stay alive. Birds, animals, insects, and fishes rely on instinct. Memory or prior training is not necessary, but the inner-knowing of instinct tells all species what to do for the first time under various conditions without prior knowledge. As wild animals grow older they learn from their species how to continue to exist. They also begin to acquire information by observation, memory, and life experiences. If circumstances change, animals can modify their behavior and adapt their strategies to survive in a changing environment.

There is growing evidence that many animals in the wild, particularly dolphins, monkeys, and birds, are handy with tools and with figuring out puzzles. Some creatures know how to use natural objects as protective tools when threatened. For example, the veined octopus has been spotted carrying two halves of empty coconut shells suctioned to their undersides. When a predator approaches the octopus can hide inside undetected. I guess this indicates that even an octopus is capable of advanced planning.

When was the last time that you made a conscious decision to try something new to improve your personal or professional circumstances? If you cannot adapt to change, you will not see the future coming. You must recognize the need for self-directed, inner changes to adapt and survive in a fast-changing world. Don't let what seems to be chance or fate decide your future. Opportunities are knocking on your door right now, but if you are too distracted to pay attention, you will exist on the edge of extinction. Your quality of life is determined by your quality of thinking. You can change your thinking and your choices if you want to modify your circumstances. What messages are the wild animals giving you? Are you ignoring something that can help you survive and adapt to changing times?

## CHAPTER SIXTEEN NOTES

# CHAPTER SEVENTEEN
# Symbols are Messages

S YMBOLS CAN BE PICTURES instead of words and offer quick, nonverbal communication. Symbols typically represent information and instruction, but they can also represent ideas, thoughts, goals, warnings, or possible upcoming events. Symbols are visual messages. For example, road signs use symbols to speak to exhausted travelers looking for rest areas, bathrooms, gas stations, campsites, and food. The simple symbol of a knife and fork is all it takes to convey the idea that a restaurant is coming up a few exits down the highway. When you are worn-out, just seeing roadside symbols can convey their suggestive values of rest, security, sleep, food, and comfort.

The history of human communication dates back before the power of the spoken word. Symbols are the human race's oldest form of communication and constitute the universal language that speaks to the human subconscious.

Every word you speak and every thought you think has its roots in your conscious mind, which gives a mental form to your ideas. A confused state of mind cannot communicate or express itself well. When you think, speak, or write, your words act as symbols for what you are trying to communicate. What words represent gives us a language so we can communicate our feelings or information to others.

On the other hand, the subconscious uses no formal language to convey knowledge to the conscious mind. Its method of communication is revealed in the tone of your voice, your gestures, behavior, actions, and feelings. Words are only the verbal expressions of your feeling. Words have no feeling in themselves, but how you respond to them creates your emotions. Information is passed through the conscious and subconscious, but words are never exchanged. Contact with persons, places, and things are made on a feeling level only, which is the universal language of the subconscious. A symbol may use no words but saves time through being direct.

Paying attention to a symbol can help you prevent an accident. Keeping your eyes on the road and avoiding distractions like cell phones and pumping up the volume of your radio while driving are crucial if you want to live another day. Another important part of driving is paying attention to warning road signs that can inform you of upcoming hazards. For example, an image of a deer crossing on a road sign can help you avoid a future accident. If you see a deer crossing sign, drive with caution. Think seriously of other important road signs or symbols you encounter daily because they can help you stay alive in the future.

## Symbols Talk to You

Symbols are universal messages that help you successfully overcome obstacles that block your mind when there is a language barrier in verbal communication. The receptive state of your subconscious is always open to suggestions and symbols that can be utilized to increase your awareness, influence situations, solve problems, and attain goals. Your attraction to a particular symbol signifies its importance in your life. Symbols are messages for your physical, mental, and emotional well-being. Your subconscious tends to use simple images to convey upcoming events that you can miss if you are not paying attention. Symbols can express your fears, expectations, desires, goals, feelings, and opinions.

Some symbols in the subconscious connect you to memories, old feelings, and thoughts that still influence your behavior today, whether you realize it or not. Symbols also offer you information and advice regarding your future. Certain images have a symbolic meaning and are the language that your higher self uses to guide and communicate intuitive knowledge. To develop your ESP powers, you must train yourself to understand the meaning behind the symbols. Take the time to analyze the symbols that appear to you on a daily basis. Some symbols may appear more often than other symbols. Your subconscious recognizes many symbols, but they are of no value to you if you ignore them. A symbol can warn you to stop, look, and listen!

## Symbols Serve as Triggers

Symbols can also be used consciously to direct or focus your thoughts, increase your energy, act as reminders, influence healing, and offer strength, guidance and protection. Any symbol that makes you feel strong and protected is of extreme suggestive value. A symbol can also be used to help you when you are physically ill or depressed. If you are feeling ill, you are temporarily detached from positive healing energy. When you are low on energy or disheartened, it is important to reconnect to meaningful symbols. Familiar objects and symbols provide positive suggestive value through your physical senses and your intuition. When you are going through trials or feel down in the dumps, use a symbol to help you increase your mental, physical, and emotional strength. This will help you reconnect with other people who share your belief in a particular symbol or faith, and this attracts beneficial energies and blessings.

Everything that you have in your home has suggestive value. Symbols can help you recall an event connected to it. That is why it is not a good idea to keep old love letters from someone you now cannot stomach. Get rid of the letters physically, and you are more likely to rid yourself of those old reminders on an emotional level as well.

All symbols can act as triggers to help you recall what they represent. The American flag is an important symbol for many people. Most Americans identify it as a symbol of freedom. Other countries have flags and symbols that have special meaning to their citizens and subjects. Christians attract a powerful healing energy from their faith in Jesus, which is symbolized in the cross. The six-pointed Star of David of the Jews and the Medicine Wheel of the Native American people are important spiritual sources of comfort and healing. Buddhism, Confucianism, Islam, and Hinduism, to name just a handful of other religions, all have their special symbols that speak to the heart and spirit of the believers.

Symbols are all around you and have great suggestive value to the human mind. The stars, the moon, and the sun are indicative of healing, warmth, and light. They remind you of your connection to the sky as well as the earth. The circle is a powerful symbol of power, protection, healing, and strength for many cultures. However, the meaning of the circle may vary according to the culture.

If you are fearful, do not allow your anxieties to control you. Maintain control of your emotions by redirecting your thinking process with symbols. Anything is possible when you use symbols to reconnect with the power of belief and faith. Do you know that you can use symbols to remind you of your appreciation for life? For example, use a birdhouse to remind you to be thankful for your home, whether it's a hut, a mansion, or a rented room. A tree can be a symbol to remind you of strength and material comfort, such as your bed and other furniture that represent security to you. Use wind chimes as symbols to help you remember to pray for yourself and other people in need of help. A bridge is a powerful symbol as a reminder that you are connected to everyone and everything.

Your subconscious is intuitive, creative, and receptive. Your conscious mind works with its physical senses and is logical. It responds to what it sees, feels, smells, hears, tastes, and so on. The subconscious records the whole experience and acts on it, bringing it into the future. A simple symbol can remind you of your goal to help you create your future. A symbol can represent the past, the present, and the future. A symbol that is emotionally charged usually has deep inner meaning for you.

**Other Significant Symbols**

Symbols could be repeated images that act as guides, signals, rituals, protection, or reminders for you to think or act in a particular manner. Once you recognize a symbol you can connect with its meaning anywhere. Some symbols have meaningful significance that applies to large groups of people. For example, early Christians used the symbol of the fish to acknowledge or identify with fellow followers of Jesus. The fish symbol did not require a verbal warning, but it was absolutely necessary to prevent capture or persecution. The fish also signaled when it was safe to talk about Jesus without being turned in or harassed by the authorities.

Symbols also had significance for the Native Americans who were prohibited by law to practice their spirituality before the Indian Religious Freedom Act was passed in 1978. The sacred Native American pipe has deep spiritual significance for its people, but because of religious persecution, the sacred pipe ceremony had to be performed in secrecy. After the blessed pipe was disassembled it was easier to conceal.

## Personal Symbols

A symbol reveals information to advise you regarding its use. Every day, countless symbols help you communicate verbally and nonverbally. A graphic may convey a nonverbal message with great efficiency, such as a no smoking sign, stop sign, or detour sign. Make it a point to really look at all the symbols that surround you on a daily basis. Any time you notice something, it notices you! You will recognize more symbols now because you are looking at them from a different perspective.

Your personal symbols will have to be interpreted according to the meaning and personal importance to you. If you dream of a dolphin, what is its significance to you? List some of your personal symbols. Can you interpret their meaning as you have come to understand them? Do some of your symbols appear more often than others? What are the symbols that get your full attention? Try to recall some symbols and how they have helped you in the past. Learn to identify the way your subconscious symbolically talks to you. Note the symbols that appear in your dreams, the shapes of clouds in the sky, and even the shapes on the palm of your hands. Look on the inner surface of your hands. Can you see circles, squares, triangles, stars, alphabets, and other symbols on your palms? What else do you see? Sometimes you can miss seeing something that is right in front of your eyes.

Do you have a scar or birthmark somewhere on your body or face? Does it have a shape? If it is a scar, can you recall the incident connected to it? Memories link you to persons, places, and things. A scar is a part of your history and tells its own story today. If you do not like the story, disconnect from it. We all have inner scars that may not be seen on the outside, though they affect us on many levels. The subconscious will try to help you recognize symbols to promote your well-being on the inside.

If you are drawn to trees, rocks, or other natural symbols, they can help you to heal old emotional pain and issues that are not for your highest good. Is there a particularly strong symbol for you? Is it something that you doodle on a piece of paper while talking on the phone? Get in touch with the symbols that are all around you because they are also within you.

## CHAPTER SEVENTEEN NOTES

# CHAPTER EIGHTEEN

# General and Premonitory Dreams

W E ALL DREAM even if we cannot recall our dreams upon awakening. Dreams have fascinated and captivated all cultures throughout the world. The Bible, Koran, Talmud, and other great books are full of discussions of dreams, including prophetic dreams that include warnings and prophecies. Jung and Freud, Nostradamus and Muhammad, and many others assigned predictive value to their dreams. Our ancestors looked to their dreams for advice, instructions, solutions, healing, answers, and warnings. People dream in modern times just as they dreamed in the ancient past.

In fact, dreaming connects you to the past, present, and future. Unknowable information appears in the mind's eye, along with other imagery, impressions, and other sources of knowledge in the dream state. Dreams can be linked to change, risk, relationships, health, career, endings, beginnings, blessings, decision-making, emotional issues, solutions, and the future. The future is determined by causes that exist as potential physical forms. These material forms may first appear in your inner-world of dreams. Your dreams can reveal the future before it comes to pass.

Although dreams in general are discussed in this chapter, I am most often asked to interpret the premonitory, forewarning dream, so this is why it is featured. As I have stated earlier in this book, my knowledge and understanding of dreams is not acquired from the study of dream interpretation, but rather from my strong intuitive sense regarding the simple premonitory dream as a forewarning of a future event or experience.

The premonitory dream can be symbolically linked to a state of mind that is influenced by recent thoughts, experiences, concerns, and feelings about your real life issues. To get the inner meaning of the symbols that appear in your premonitory dreams they must be linked to your current or recent life challenges which have triggered the warning. However, the forewarning dream can also be taken as face value, just as it appears in the following example.

### Lily-Therese has a Premonitory Dream

Many people report accurate premonitory dreams of unknown events. Even when you are unable to make sense of your dream at the time, it is wise to record it for future reference. If you can see the future in a dream, you can intervene to prevent it from happening or encourage it to occur.

I had such a dream several years ago and was able to prevent what I saw by intervening. In my dream, I waited for the bus to take me to work. To get a better view of the coming bus, I stood on top of the bus bench. When I saw no bus in sight, I sat down again. For some unknown reason I began feeling very apprehensive. While I was trying to decide on the cause of my gut feelings, a green pickup truck driven by a drunk driver crashed next to my bench.

I woke up immediately. The dream felt so real that I wrote it down, and I was so anxious that I purchased a used car to drive to work from then on. About one year later, my car clutch went out, so I took the bus to work. I remembered my dream so I stood several feet away from the bus bench. I understood that my anxiety was actually a strong warning from my subconscious that, if I did not heed the forewarning in my dream, there was a strong probability of its happening in my physical world. Just as I was ready to laugh at myself for being so jumpy, a green pickup truck came out of nowhere and crashed into the bus bench, killing the drunken driver instantly. The dream allowed me to see this event in advance, and I was able to prevent it from happening.

## Prepare the Mind to Recall Dreams

Before going to sleep, clear your mind of your earlier concerns and let go of fears and uncertainty. It is possible through positive suggestion to prepare the mind to receive information, instruction, guidance, and solutions through your dreams, so put aside your negative experiences of the day. You must let go of your emotional issues, or they will take forms as nightmares. Sometimes it is helpful to go over your day and create an elimination list prior to going to bed. Writing down your worries will help you to let go of them consciously. A clear mind frees your subconscious to receive intuitive insight to protect and guide you. When you consciously think of a particular problem, your dreams will try to assist you in finding a resolution.

Some of your dreams may be puzzling or mysterious. Other dreams may appear to be some tell-all book of your history. Deep, dark secrets, bad choices, and negative habits may come to the surface like skeletons from your closet. If the subconscious is overloaded it will attempt to clean out and organize the conscious mind to better communicate with you.

You know what happens when your computer is overloaded on your hard drive. It crashes. Do not try to bury your secrets, or they will continue to come back in other scary nightmares that may even be exaggerated to get your attention. Face your fears in the light of day, and allow your conscious mind to cast them out with your new understanding of cause and effect. Remember, your past is not who you are now. Bless your past because without your earlier experiences you would not be the person you are today.

Release negative emotions associated with your daily experiences. If you have a major concern to which you would like a solution, look at the problem from several different angles before going to sleep The solution to your problems may be revealed in the form of symbols in your dreams or in the omens, signs, and coincidences that may catch your eye the following days. Your desire for a solution attracts persons, places, and things that have the answer you are seeking. It is important to keep your mind open and receptive to all information coming through. Ask for help, and then accept it no matter what form it takes. Try to keep your emotions out of your dream interpretations. If you fear a particular outcome, you could block out whatever information is available. Dreams are influenced by your daily life experiences and emotional state. Learn to detach from negative emotions that try to control you, such as anger, fear, resentment, and hate. Releasing negative emotions can help you interpret your dreams more accurately because you will have less mental and emotional garbage to sort through.

If you have been worrying about a particular situation, your subconscious will try to help you find a solution. When you sleep, the conscious mind shuts down and the subconscious is able to provide you with information, guidance, and instruction. You can receive the outcome of situations if you pay attention to what the subconscious has to tell you about your concerns and fears. Most of the time you may not pay attention to your dreams or forget about them, but if the dream is really disturbing it will grab your attention. If you continue to ignore your dream, it will recur, sometimes in exaggerated form. Take time to analyze your dreams and listen to your inner self. Make it a practice to stop, look, and listen to frightening, dangerous warning or threatening dreams. Any dream that seems to predict the future should get your attention even if it makes no sense at the time.

Immediately upon waking, write down your dreams or record them before you forget the details. Many of your dreams may contain symbols, animals, unusual behavior, and even strange creatures that you must learn to interpret. Colors are also important in dreams. Important dreams may appear in color or black and white. I have found that dreams pertaining to myself are usually in black and white. When my dreams are about other people, they are always in vivid color. Dreams have helped me prepare for the future.

**Dreams Offer a Treasure Chest of Information**
To deny the benefits of dreams is to deny your own treasure chest of blessings. You should look at dreams as resources of knowledge, healing, advice, revelations, and assistance. Your dreams can help you understand your daily experiences, while providing you with knowledge of the future. Reviewing your dreams when troubles confront you will often give you a sense of control and intervention.

Dreams are usually personal, but they can also pertain to family, friends, pets, enemies, and even global issues. You are most often the best interpreter of your dreams. Many times, you may not understand the meaning of your dreams because you are not in touch with how your subconscious talks to you. You may try to ignore the dream, but, if it is important, you will be unable to dismiss it easily from your mind.

For some of you, dreaming is the only method your subconscious has to give you important information because it is easier to receive ESP information when the conscious mind is shut down and no longer blocking your intuitive self. Dreaming gives you immediate access to a realm where the limitations of the physical world of the conscious mind do not exist. Physical time and space, the past and the future do not exist in the dream world. The mind loses its logic and reasoning abilities and an intuitive sense is turned on. Since there are no boundaries or restrictions when you dream, there is a certain amount of letting go. With freedom comes the awakening of the potential that exists within each one of you to understand your predictable future.

Many creative people have found that a problem was solved in a dream in a manner unlike their ordinary way of thinking. Famous people, such as, Albert Einstein, Benjamin Franklin and Thomas Edison were all known to take their problems or important decisions to bed with them for answers and solutions. Dynamic people throughout history have credited their unique ideas, creations and inventions to their dreams.

People living all over the world have received guidance, suggestions, ideas, answers, inventions, instruction, and solutions from their dreams. What the conscious mind denies, the subconscious accepts. Be on good terms with your subconscious, and it will not desert you. It will provide you with an abundance of wisdom and guidance. You will receive information that is truly predictive and may even save your life. Some dreams, especially nightmares, may be connected to a physical condition, but they may also predict possible future events or experiences.

In some dreams, dreamers may have superpowers. Dreamers have access to everyone and everything because of our telepathic connection to the Universal Consciousness. Dreams provide a variety of information that can help you look at things from many different perspectives. Learn to interpret your dreams within the realm of possibilities. If you dream of winning the lottery, try to control yourself by purchasing only one ticket. Buying fifty tickets will not increase your chances of winning big. Your dreams may reveal your deep hopes and desires, but use common sense when your dreams reveal negative solutions to solving your money problems. Robbing a bank will do you no good if you are behind bars.

Your dreams can also correspond to your ideas of reality, so use your personal everyday experiences when you interpret them. When you learn to interpret your dreams, you will have access to information that can heal, bless, and save you. Dreams sometimes use familiar people, living or dead, to get through to you. You will usually pay more attention to someone that you know than a stranger. However, at times it's the strangers that provide you with the most information. Also, consider a stranger as a possible part of you that is unrecognized or missing from your conscious mind. In the mysterious world of dreams, you have magical powers, elephants talk, inanimate objects have opinions, and owls give advice. Nothing is too far out in a dream because the rules of reality do not apply.

## What Nightmares Reveal

When you are too distracted by your outer-world, nightmares shock you into paying attention to your inner-world. Nightmares symbolize your deepest fears and emotional issues in frightening imagery you cannot ignore. Nightmares are the alarms and sirens of the dream world. Nightmares warn of problems you need to solve in your everyday world. If you seriously hurt a body part in your physical world, it gets your attention and you go to an emergency hospital immediately. In your dreams, nightmares will shout at you to get help because you are disconnected on some level from your inner-self and the help it can provide.

If you require physical or psychological help, your subconscious will try to alert you of things hidden beneath the surface of your conscious mind. Nightmares can be very frightening, but they can also alert you to disturbing issues that need your attention. Some nightmares may contain warnings or knowledge of things yet to come. Other nightmares are symbolic expressions of the subconscious as it puzzles out your life experiences. Stress, anxiety, change, relationships, work issues, health, risk, and other internal conflicts may be linked to very upsetting nightmares. A nightmare can offer insight regarding coming times or health issues.

See if you can pick up some of the symbols in the following nightmare.

## Florence Escapes the Jaws of Deception

When Florence initially met Jack, she had just received a large amount of money from a lawsuit settlement. Florence was so thrilled that she mentioned the money to Jack, who promptly did a double take and turned on the charm. Jack had just started a new business, and he needed investors. He was an outspoken man and did not beat around the bush when it came to asking people for money. After just two months of dating, Jack suggested that Florence invest some of her money in his new business. He requested the currency in cash—in hundred dollar bills, no less! Florence said that she would think about it.

A month went by with nothing from his new potential investor. Florence was taking too long to make up her mind about the investment. *Hmm,* Jack thought. *I have to come up with a scheme fast to get that cash.* Two days later, Jack threw out the bait by giving Florence a bouquet of red roses. Over dinner and a couple of glasses of wine, Jack came on strong to Florence. Jack said that it was time to put his bachelor days behind him and settle down with the right woman. He looked meaningful into Florence's eyes to imply that the lucky woman was her.

That did it, and Florence was hooked. She agreed to make a $10,000 investment. However, that night she got cold feet and felt nauseas, so she reconsidered her decision. *Who knows when the next money settlement may come around?* She thought. She was sure that Jack was not the winning ticket to her financial security.

Florence thought and thought about her dilemma, and she worried. She felt trapped by her agreement. She definitely did not want to make the cash investment, so her friend the subconscious came up with more gut-level warnings, and even an answer in the form of a scary nightmare. Florence's dream was bloodcurdling, but it offered a solution. Florence saw herself at the bottom of an ancient pit toilet being chased by a large, angry, hungry crocodile.

She wondered how this large reptile could fit into such a small space. Florence instinctively knew that she had to do something fast or the crocodile would devour her whole. She could hear the *chomp, chomp* of its huge, greedy jaws getting closer. While Florence was worrying about what to do in her desperate situation, her "alarm" clock unexpectedly went off loudly. Oh, what a relief it was to hear the alarm go off instead of her head! Florence woke up fearful, but she felt relieved.

Florence was now wide awake; she recognized the red flag and took action immediately. Florence met Jack in a coffeehouse to tell him that she had changed her mind about investing in his company. When she gave Jack the news, his jaw dropped wide open like the crocodile's in complete astonishment. What's more, he had dressed for this special occasion wearing shoes and a belt made from crocodile skin!

Florence was not surprised and instantly made the connection to her nightmare. This was no "Crocodile Dundee" twist of fate. Jack stood up and angrily told Florence that she was not good enough to share his life. Florence said, "Thank you," and left the restaurant feeling wiser and much richer.

How would you interpret this nightmare? Write down the symbols and their meaning to you. This is a very helpful exercise to zero in on your issues because it reveals how the subconscious acts on your behalf and responds to your request for help. It is always easier to see someone else's mistakes, but doing this exercise can reveal what you are not seeing or avoiding in your own life.

## A Premonitory Dream Saves Johnny's Life

We may experience premonitions in dreams, visions, or strong feelings that foretell of a future event without a logical explanation. Our ability to survive depends on our subconscious, so it will try to warn us of coming threats through our emotions and hunches. Although we may not identify them on a conscious level, our premonitions cause us to make unconscious choices. We cancel our airplane flight only to find out later that the plane crashed. For example, a man decided to take a car instead of an airplane just two hours before the plane was scheduled to take off. Johnny was planning to travel by plane with two of his closest friends to a skiing resort, but he cancelled because of a strong premonitory dream and his gut feelings. Unfortunately, the plane crashed killing both of his companions. When he was asked about his sudden change of plans he replied, "Last night I dreamt about a plane crash. The closer it came to our departure time, the more uneasy I became, so I cancelled because of my dream and something did not feel right."

A true premonition will get stronger and stronger as time passes, but if it is not an authentic warning it will simply disappear over time.

Premonitions are sometimes based on internal clues that we don't always recognize, but we feel. A true gut-level feeling can be an instant instinctive response requiring no thinking on our part, only feelings that make us act on them.

There are numerous accounts of premonitory dreams. Foreknowledge of approaching death in dreams is not that unusual. President Lincoln had a dream of his own death while living in the White House. The president saw himself dead and lying in state in the East Room. When he was assassinated, the accuracy of his dream was confirmed. Before President Kennedy was assassinated, many people had premonitions of his impending death, including me. Some dreams challenge your preconceptions and logical explanations regarding your physical world. The interpretation of dreams is very important, but acting on them is even more significant!

### Randy Should Have Listened to his Dream

Randy was scheduled to go on a business trip the following morning. The night before his trip, he dreamed that he was killed in a car accident. When he woke up, he told his wife of his dream, but decided that the trip was necessary so, against his better judgment, he went anyway. Coming back from his business trip, he was killed instantly when a drunk driver collided with his vehicle.

### Henry Sees his Unfortunate Future, but ignores it

Henry had a realistic dream that scared him so badly he woke up. In his dream, he saw himself lying in a dark gray casket. He was wearing a charcoal gray suit, a light gray dress shirt, and a burgundy necktie. A young woman dressed in dark clothing stood next to his open casket. She was crying softly into a black lacy handkerchief. In his dream, he watched as his body was escorted out of the church by the unknown woman and three other mourners. He listened to the *click* and *clack* of the coffin as it rolled down the center of the church aisle. Henry could hear someone asking, "Why?"

Then he realized he had awakened and he was the one asking the question out loud. He was sweating profusely from his gut-level feeling of dread, and he was unable to go back to sleep. The next morning at breakfast, he described his nightmare in detail to his brother. The dream upset him, but he was only thirty-two years old, single, and in good health. Henry was an attorney so he tried not to leave anything to chance. He had an insurance policy naming his brother Paul as the beneficiary.

One year later, while on a business trip in a Spain, Henry fell madly in love with a beautiful hot-blooded senorita named Maria. After a whirl-wind romance, they married. He was planning to move his beautiful new bride to New York, when he was killed in a traffic accident. His new wife sadly informed his brother of his death. Six weeks later in an intuitive session with me, Paul recalled Henry's dream. His question to me was, "Should I put in a claim for the $100,000 insurance policy?" He told me that he felt guilty about the circumstances.

Say what? I told him to make an insurance claim immediately. Paul never did update me when everything was settled, but I did hear through the grapevine that he was kicking up his heels in Jamaica.

## Christina Did the Right Thing

Christina" was planning to visit a daughter in Oklahoma for two weeks. Three days before she left for her destination, she had a dream in which she was making out her will. Christina was in good health and only for-ty-two years old. However, she felt so strongly about this neglected mat-ter that she had planned on making a will upon her return trip home. However, the dream made her feel so uneasy that the very next day she decided to make a will before leaving for her journey. While waiting for her daughter to pick her up from the airport, Christina was killed by a vehicle with no brakes.

## Anna Identifies a Killer in a Dream

Anna dreamed that she visited her daughter Rose, whom she had not seen in three years. She and her daughter had not communicated for all that time because Rose has a history of choosing men with criminal histories of whom Anna did not approve.

In her dream, she approached the front door of her daughter's house and knocked. A tall, heavy-set man in his mid-fifties opened the door. He had beady eyes nearly hidden behind round, thick glasses. He kept adjust-ing them. His salt-and-pepper hair was thinning, but he sported a thick handlebar mustache that covered his upper lip. He wore a black t-shirt with a white skull on the front. The man appeared to be nervous, agitated, and surprised.

When Anna started asking questions, the man became rude and slammed the door in her face. As Anna walked back to her car, she looked at the address on the mailbox again. It read, *11000 Sunset Street*. She woke up feeling very anxious.

After her dream, Anna decided to put the past behind her. Anna sent a letter to her daughter's last known address, which was not the address of her dream. After waiting a month for a reply, she sent another letter. After waiting yet another month with no reply, Anna contacted the police. After much questioning, the authorities requested a DNA sample from Anna. After more investigation, Anna was told that her daughter had been murdered the previous year and the case was still unsolved. The police had been unable to notify the next of kin because the information was unavailable.

With a heavy heart and many tears, Anna told the police that she knew where they could find her daughter's killer. Three days later, they arrested the man of Anna's dream at the address she had seen on the mailbox. The man looked exactly as she had seen him. The man had killed her daughter when she threatened to report him to the police for robbery and other illegal activities. In a drunken rage he choked Rose to death. He then buried her body in a shallow grave in an empty lot. Children playing in the lot discovered the grave. Before the body's discovery, he gave all of their personal belongings to someone who did not ask questions. He immediately moved to a new address in a different state. The dream had accurately reported his new address.

## Lily-Therese Sees the Future

I had a very unusual premonitory dream about forty years ago. I was unable to get a good night's sleep the previous evening, so I decided to take a nap in the afternoon. Before too long I was sleeping soundly. In my dream, I saw a murder take place. Two men argued over a matter that I was not able to hear in my dream. I saw one man turn around to leave the area, and then the second man hit him over the head with a crowbar several times. In my dream, I could not see myself, but what I had seen was enough for me. I was getting ready to leave the scene when the second man turned around and looked directly at me. I then woke up. The hands on the clock pointed to 5:00 p.m. I was very relieved that it was only a dream. I closed my eyes but was unable to go back to sleep.

About six months later while giving Steve an intuitive counseling session, I had a very strong gut feeling. About midway through the session, I became very uneasy. In disbelief, I recognized the second man of my dream and recalled the whole nightmare instantly. I was shocked, and for a few moments I just stared at the man. Feeling as though I was in a trance and unable to stop myself, I told Steve that I knew his secret. He and I looked at each other for what seemed like ages. Steve continued to stare and, to break the connection, I looked at the clock. The hands of the clock pointed to 5:00 p.m. After a couple of more intense moments, Steve took a deep breath and then told me that he had also seen me in a dream. I believe he said a bad dream.

Steve proceeded to tell me what happened on that fateful day. Steve told me that his wife had left him when he accused her of having an affair with their mutual friend, Tim. Millie denied it, but packed her clothes the very same day and "got out of Dodge." However, when Steve accused Tim, he admitted to the affair, shrugged his shoulders, and turned around to leave. The rest is history.

Since this incident, Tim had been haunting him. When Steve told a friend of the haunting, the friend suggested that he make an appointment to see me. This professional referral was no out of the blue coincidence, but I simply did not know enough to assign a cause to this unusual chain of events. I have to admit that some events and experiences are unexplainable. I was amazed how accurately my earlier dream had predicted the future. Indeed, I was surprised. However, after countless years of experiencing the unusual, I confess that I was not totally shocked.

I took a flash forward look into Steve's future. I told Steve that guilt was keeping Tim earthbound and trapped in the physical world. In addition, guilt was responsible for keeping Steve emotionally tied to the victim. Forgiveness on both sides was the only solution and method of release. I suggested that he turn himself in to the police for the crime, which he eventually did.

The past influences the present and future. What goes around does, without a doubt, come back around. I will never forget this experience.

## Kimberly has a Premonitory Dream

Premonitory dreams can recur and warn you of coming times. Reoccurring dreams will continue until they get your complete attention. You must act on the information if you are to benefit from your premonitory dreams. The key word here is act. Remember, procrastination can kill.

Several years ago, Kimberly had a dream that saved her life. In this premonitory, reoccurring dream, my client saw herself lying in bed. She was wearing a bright pink nightgown, and her hair was tied in a ponytail. She was tossing and turning in an obvious nightmare. In the dream, she suddenly sat up in bed just moments before the bedroom ceiling fan came crashing down, barely missing her. The room began to shake violently, and objects begin to fly off the wall. In her dream, Kimberly immediately jumped out of bed. She woke up trembling and sweating.

Kimberly had problems sleeping after this nightmare, but it was not until her second reoccurring dream that she began to be concerned. By the time she experienced the third reoccurring nightmare, she was a nervous wreck. That did it. At last, she did a phone consultation with me regarding her nightmares. Kimberly talked as rapidly as an auctioneer, and my impression was that she moved like a fast-striking electrical storm. She held a powerful position in her corporation, but in the business world she was well known for her emotional storms. Kimberly had a mouth that roared like thunder and an attitude to match it. She put out the fire of enthusiasm on many business meetings. Team spirit was definitively not one of her strong points, but she excelled at intimidation. And these were only my first impressions!

I had Kimberly relax over the telephone and I closed my eyes. I compared my initial mental impressions with my gut-level feelings to connect with her energy. I immediately felt my hair stand straight up from my head as I received a charge of static electricity. I definitely could feel a strong, uncontrolled, electrical force in her energy field. In some cases, the human aura can take on the characteristics of the natural elements because we are a part of nature. In fact, some people claim to attract unwelcome electrical storms and lightning on a regular basis. Could this be the outcome of an unrecognized subconscious cause?

Our magnetic energy field could attract the temperament of our thinking and return it in some physical form that corresponds to our disposition. The personal temperament of the individual will often reveal the form this energy will take. Kimberly's reoccurring nightmare told me that a destructive outcome was already in motion. I was happy to report that, since it had not yet occurred, Kimberly could intervene by leaving her mobile home as soon as possible.

Kimberly listened to what I had to say, but I do not know if she heard me. Kimberly really needed to relax, calm down, and let go of her control issues. I suggested meditation, yoga, exercise, and some release work.

Kimberly decided to take no chances so she made immediate plans to visit a cousin in Arizona. Six days later during a very bad, unexpected Louisiana hurricane, a portion of a tree hit by lightning came crashing through her bedroom ceiling. The ceiling fan was broken into pieces in the middle of her bed, joined by a large twisted tree branch. Broken glass and busted furniture were all over the place.

What would have been the outcome if Kimberly had not paid attention to the reoccurring dream? Kimberly moved like a storm to another state to avoid hurricanes, but I do not know if she ever connected her emotional storms to her past programming. If she has made no changes in her thinking, her energy field could possibly attract another such incident. Although her dream did not prevent the disaster from occurring, it saved her life. The premonitory dream was a direct warning from her subconscious that took the outward appearance of a reoccurring dream. The dream was a definite warning to prepare for the unexpected, no matter what form it took.

**Trust in your Dreams**

Trust in your dreams and intuition. Act on information that appears to be a warning, no matter how silly it sounds to the conscious mind. Respect your extra-sensory abilities, and they will not fail you. If you experience a recurring dream, pay close attention and get professional help in its interpretation if you need it.

The constant, endless babble of your conscious mind will block out the wisdom of the subconscious. The voice of intuition is only heard in silence, but instinct is felt in your physical body as a strong urge to take immediate action. Sometimes, the only time you can silence the mind is when it shuts down in sleep. When there is silence, the subconscious takes advantage of its freedom from the conscious mind and issues its warnings, predictions, and guidance. Pay attention to what is going on in your life in the daytime, and you will be in a better position to understand your nighttime dreams. Dreams will try to provide you with solutions and answers to your most difficult problems.

## Lucid Dreaming and the Future

Lucid dreams occur when dreamers realize they are dreaming. You usually have control in a lucid dream and can participate consciously in your dream. However, in some lucid dreams dreamers may be aware that they are dreaming but are unable to control the outcome of the dream. Colors are vivid, and the physical senses are fully awakened. You can see, smell, taste, hear, and feel in a lucid dream. Anything can happen in this kind of a dream and usually does. You can fly like a bird, talk to the dead, or become a world-famous rock star instantly.

## Lily-Therese Meets Big Jack

As a child, I once was able to avoid a serious problem by remembering my lucid dream. In this particular dream, a large, black, barking dog chased me down a muddy path. All of my physical senses were seriously engaged as I ran for my life. I was fully aware of my every action in my lucid dream. I could smell the mud as I kicked it up with my bare feet. I could hear the dog panting as it pursued me down an unfamiliar, narrow path. I never knew that I could run so fast, but I was highly motivated.

My eyes begin to search for a safe place to hide. I approached a run-down barn that looked like it would fall apart with the next strong wind. On top of the barn, a crooked, metal weathervane shaped like a running horse monitored the wind. Next to an aged hen house, several chickens scratched the ground for insects, snails, and worms. A scrawny red rooster perched on top of a fence post kept watch over his hens. He appeared edgy and was obviously watching out for predators. This rooster clearly ruled the roost, but he lost control when the hens scattered as soon as they heard me shrieking.

About seventy-five feet from the barn stood an old house that had seen better days. A large calico cat slept on top of a corroded shed undisturbed by my commotion. I decided immediately to run to the barn because it was closer. I ducked down low, hoping that Stephen King's monster dog Cujo would not see me, but he immediately spotted me.

I attempted to get away, but I tripped over an old rusty tool that was half-hidden in the ground. Before I could get up, Cujo began nipping at my legs. I closed my eyes, covered my face with my hands, and froze. I could smell the putrid breath of the dog as saliva dripped from its mouth. When I finally got enough nerve to open my eyes again, the dog's head was right in front of my face. Yikes! I could count nearly all of its teeth, and, boy, were they sharp! I played dead like a possum and eventually heard someone calling his name, Big Jack, to come home. After barking at me for a few more moments, the angry dog ran in the direction of the angry voice. What a relief to know that it was only a dream!

Two weeks later while playing outside in an adventurous mood, I decided to take a walk. I saw my mother hanging clothes outside. I decided not to disturb her by asking her for permission to leave our property. As soon as I was out of sight, I removed my socks and shoes. I began to jump in puddles as it had rained the night before. Out of nowhere, a wild rabbit appeared right in front of me. *Oh my, Br'er Rabbit*, I thought. How impressed my mother would be with my catch for dinner! The rabbit had other ideas and was much faster than I. It ran zigzag and eventually escaped into a dense thicket. When I stopped running I discovered that I was lost. Yet something about the marshy area was familiar, and my gut feelings put me on high alert.

I looked anxiously around me and spied the very same dog of my nightmare, though twice as large and three times uglier. It was observing me next to a moss covered tree that stood about seventy-five feet behind me. I recalled my dream as fast as I could in my desperate situation and decided to run.

*Which way?* I wondered. *Which way?* All of a sudden, my eyes were attracted to an old rusty mailbox with its red flag up. The mailbox was unimpressive, but to me it stood out like a lighthouse beckoning help and protection. The heat was on, so I choose that direction to run. Just beyond some moss-covered trees were the barn and the house of my nightmare. I already knew the outcome if I went to the barn, so I ran directly to the house, which I banged loudly on the door and yelled at the top of my lungs. Within seconds, the door was yanked open by a tall, thin, older woman wearing a long black dress, a dark gray apron, and an old-fashioned black bonnet. This was the common clothing for women in mourning in the 1940s. The lady lost no time in grabbing me by my arm and pulled me into the house. She ran into the kitchen and looked out the dusty window pane. I followed her, but I was too short to see out the window so I quickly pulled up a chair and stood on top of it.

The two of us saw that the dog had gotten side-tracked by the agitated chickens. The highly nervous calico cat had lost no time in running up a large cypress tree. The jumpy rooster and squawking chickens scattered in all directions. After a few angry growls at the cat, the barking dog ran to the window, stood up on its hind legs, and placed it muddy paws on the window ledge. The dog stared at us and growled deeply in its throat. Feeling brave behind the windowpane that separated us, I stuck out my tongue, but a pinch on my arm discouraged me from further expressing my feelings. The curtains were quickly drawn, and I was pulled away from the window rather abruptly.

The dog remained at the window intimidating us until he responded to an angry voice that yelled at him to go home. The woman, Madam Maude, told me that the terrifying dog belonged to her new neighbor, Big Buck, who was just as disagreeable as his dog. The dog's name was, guess what?

I was driven home by Madam Maude's niece in a beat-up pick-up truck. I was escorted without ceremony to my front door. I was afraid to face my mother, but after reconsidering, I decided to tell her my story, or at least a part of it. I recall her telling me, "I told you so," right before giving me a spanking. Three days later, Big Jack was captured after he attacked twin girls playing in their backyard. I am a dog lover, but I have to admit that I did not shed one tear over Big Jack. After the dog's capture, I resumed my old activities of wandering off to explore nature, but I always avoided Big Buck, if I saw him first.

## More Warning Dreams About the Future

In the dream-state, it is difficult to discern a possible connection with reality because things may appear to be altered. Remember, in dreams, everything takes place in present time. There is no past or future in the dream state. When you attempt to analyze your dreams, you put dreams into some kind of order to determine the time of a future occurrence.

Pay attention to possible forewarnings in dreams that involve you and other people so you may avoid many problems. Your dreams may predict future illness, personal problems, accidents, endings, and losses. Your dreams may also predict work promotions, marriages, gifts, money, lottery numbers, and other blessings. Sometimes what appears to be bad is really a good blessing in disguise to get your attention. Your dreams can give you another perception of reality from a completely unrecognized source.

## Lily-Therese and the Car Warning Dream

Most warning dreams are not actual threats to your physical survival, but some can be. Once I had a dream that I was in a car accident in which I was badly hurt. The car that I was driving was a light blue color. When I woke up, I went over the dream but decided that it did not apply to me because I did not own a light blue car. In fact, at that time I did not own a car at all. Two months later, I attended a party with a good friend. My friend drank too much and went to sleep. I looked for her car keys but could not locate them. The hostess offered me her second car to drive home, which I accepted gladly. However, when I went to the garage to take the car I noticed that it was a light blue color. Needless to say, I did not borrow her car because I knew that the risk was just too great.

## Dream Details Can Predict the Future

The next time that you are forewarned in a dream, pay attention to the obvious message but do not overlook small details. To help you predict a time period, notice how you are dressed in your dream. Do you now have a different hair cut or style from what you saw in your dream? Is your hair a different color? What about your physical body, does it look different? Who else was in your dream? Pay attention to body language and gestures. What about your emotions? Were you sad, glad, or mad? What did you hear? In your dream, your imagined physical senses will continue to provide you with helpful information. Check out small details. Do not overlook obvious information. Do not trust yourself to remember your dreams when you wake up. Train yourself to wake up and record your dreams. Writing in a dream journal will help you become more aware of your dreams and train your mind to recall them later.

You can program your dreams to provide you with information about the future. Most dreams that contain such information may appear quite real. You may know that you are dreaming, but you may not physically appear in your dreams. I have had several dreams that have come true. In fact, most of the ESP that has come true for me has come through my dreams. I rely on precognitive dreams. I find such dreams amazing and accurate.

## Janet Remembers a Dream

William once told me of a dream involving his cousin Janet. In the dream, he saw Janet wearing a heavy navy blue hoodie with blue jeans, black boots, black gloves, and a long, red, knitted scarf. She was running away from a large mountain lion. Since both cousins lived in an overpopulated city in New York, this was highly improbable. William dismissed his dream, but the nightmare had so much detail that he mentioned it to Janet the next time that he saw her. Janet laughed, but the nightmare invoked her primal fears on a subconscious level.

Five years later, Janet felt madly in love and moved with her man, Martin, to Northern Canada near a large forest. Martin was a professional nature photographer. He prided himself on having the latest photo equipment to capture wildlife in its natural habitats.

Janet was not really into nature, but she was thrilled to have Martin "bring home the bacon" through the eye of his camera. She passed the time knitting beautiful scarves and matching hats, which she sold to satisfied customers.

One day while outside, Janet spotted a large Canadian lynx sitting on the top of the hood of her parked truck. The large feline was watching her intently. After her initial shock, her first impulse was to shoo it away. However, she remembered her cousin's dream in a flash and looked down. She was wearing the same clothing that her cousin had reported in his dream. That did it! Her cousin had mentioned a cougar, but the lynx was close enough. Lynx normally keep away from people, so the danger of confronting it was real. Janet was able to avoid a serious altercation by paying attention to her cousin's dream.

Do not discredit your dreams because they do not pertain to your present circumstances or contain odd symbols. Nature makes use of what is available in current times. Remember I said that noting your physical appearance in your dreams can hint at a time period in which it will come true? In this case it was right on!

## The Lynx has a Personal Message for Janet

It is rare to see a lynx in the daytime. It is even more remarkable to observe a lynx sitting on the hood of a truck. This strongly indicated that the wild animal had a personal message for Janet. A wild animal that reveals itself to you links you to your basic instincts, and your deeply-rooted connection to nature and omens. The sudden appearance of an animal (even if it is in a dream) can give you laser-like insight into your life in a flash.

The lynx is a silent watcher and a witness to things that are hidden beneath the surface of the subconscious. The message of the lynx to Janet may indicate that it is time to get in touch with the power of her deep inner knowledge and hidden talents. The lynx moves silently beyond time and space where dreams live. Thus the appearance of the lynx communicates another important symbolic message to Janet. This is a signal for Janet to pay attention to future dreams for indications of coming circumstances and events in her life.

I would also suggest that Janet look into the symbolic meaning of the cougar because this is the wild animal that appeared in her cousin's dream. An important point is that Janet did not ignore the warning just because the lynx appeared in reality instead of the cougar that appeared in the dream. One must be able to adapt to changing times, changing animal species, and changing conditions. To do so requires a conscious attentiveness to feelings, events, omens, and messages that may be communicated in both literal and symbolic ways.

Janet should definitely spend more time in nature. Of course, the appearance of the lynx could also indicate that some of Janet's past dark secrets are ready to come out of her closet. The lynx is the keeper of secrets but sometimes the cat comes out of the bag and tells everything! Ouch!

## Lily-Therese Recalls a Strange Warning

Here is a warning message I received in a dream. I was driving on a California freeway at about 10 p.m. I planned on turning at the next service station exit to fill up my gas tank. As I approached the exit, I saw a huge sign that really confused me. It read, Do not stop here for gas. I thought that someone was playing a joke, so I continued driving. Soon I read another sign. It read, *Danger, do not stop here for gas.* After this, I did not stop for gas. I continued driving even though my gas meter read *empty*, and I made it safely to my destination. I woke up with an uneasy gut feeling. Out of curiosity three days later, I went back to the freeway, but, of course, I saw no signs warning, *do not stop here for gas.*

About four months later, at about 10 p.m., I was driving down the same freeway and remembered my dream in a flash. I had intended to stop for gas, but as soon as I remembered my dream, I stepped on the gas pedal. The following day I learned that the same gas station that I had planned on stopping to refuel was robbed. The station attendant was badly beaten. Thank God that I paid attention to my dream!

## Lily-Therese's Premonitory/Lucid Dream

The following dream is an excellent example of a really unusual promontory and lucid dream I had as a child. In my dream, I heard someone calling my name from outside my bedroom window. I woke up, went to the window, and looked outside. It was dark and raining lightly. In a few moments, my eyes grew accustomed to the darkness, and I saw a young, dark-haired girl dressed all in white looking back at me. The dress she wore appeared to be a First Holy Communion dress, and she had a long white veil on her head. She was about nine or ten and very pretty.

After we stared at each other for a few moments, she took a few steps backward and motioned for me to follow her. I lifted up the window and stepped out. The ground was wet and cold, but I did not consider getting a coat or shoes. The sky looked ominous, and the sounds of the night were everywhere. I shivered and followed the girl into the yawning night. We passed huge oak trees draped with Spanish moss that looked like bearded old men. Every time the wind blew, their long, tenacious fingers appeared to reach out for me, chilling me to the bone.

Oh! Oh! What was the meaning of this dream, I wondered? I felt that I was right there, experiencing every moment in time.

We passed an old cemetery that screamed of death, destruction, and decay. We moved on in the darkness, and the shadows soon swallowed us up. After much walking, we finally came to our destination, a section of rural houses in south Louisiana. A large magnolia tree stood in front of the house with huge, white, fragrant flowers. To the right of the house stood one lone oak tree, draped with Spanish moss that moved like long shadows of funeral crepe.

The girl pointed to the tree. Looking up, I saw a black-bordered death notice tacked to the tree. The young girl became a little agitated when I was unable to read the notice because of wet smudges caused by the rain. The girl did not speak, once again pointed to the house, and began walking toward it. She motioned me to follow, and I did. As I drew closer to the house, I noticed a black wreath on the front door, signifying a death in the home. Before I was able to approach the house, I awoke with a start.

Before the days of the funeral parlor, it was the custom for the dead to lie in state in the family home. When a death occurred, a notice of the death, name of the deceased, and other important details appeared on a black-bordered announcement poster. The information was hand-written and tacked to trees and other prominent locations. The notices also appeared in church announcements, on storefronts, and wherever else they were permitted. Obituary notices placed in the newspaper were also available. Usually, the notices appeared only in the neighborhood of the deceased. However, if the deceased were an important person in the community, notices were placed outside the neighborhood as well. All funeral services were conducted from the home, so it was not unusual to encounter death while one was growing up. In fact, at times it was common to see death notices tacked to trees and black wreaths on the doors of homes in rural Louisiana in the 1940s.

One morning while on my way to school, I saw a line of people waiting to enter a house marked by a black-bordered wreath at the entryway. There were beautiful, fragrant magnolias in bloom in front of the home. I stopped for a few minutes out of curiosity. I was amazed to see the girl of my dream standing in line. The girl was crying, but no one paid any attention to her. I observed her for a few moments before deciding to talk to her. I remembered that I could not help her in my dream. I approached her cautiously and asked what her name was and why was she crying. She did not appear to recognize me from the dream.

She told me that her name was Angelique and she was crying because a young girl had died. The people standing in line were going to the dead girl's home to say goodbye and pay their respects to the family. The next day was the girl's funeral, and Angelique wanted to say good-bye before the girl was buried. She asked me if I would go in with her to say farewell. I said that I would, and she handed me a large magnolia flower to place in the girl's casket, as that was the dead girl's favorite flower.

I felt like I was once more in a dream. I was younger than Angelique, so I wondered how I could help her. I called upon my guardian angel for help, and I felt much better after a few moments. I soothed Angelique as best I could. I told her that we could pray for the young girl to help her get to Heaven, and she agreed to pray with me. I closed my eyes and prayed. After a few moments, I opened my eyes, but my new friend was gone. I could not see her anywhere. I decided to get back in line anyway, thinking that Angelique would turn up again and join me.

When it was my turn to approach the girl's casket, I did and looked in. I was shocked speechless to see my new friend, Angelique, lying in the casket and dressed in a First Communion dress. My legs became weak, and I nearly fainted. I had to be assisted into another room to sit down until I regained my composure. Someone gave me a glass of water, and several people asked me what happened, but I was unable to share my experience with them. I did find out later that the young dead girl's name was Angelique.

I did not attend school that day. As soon as I returned home, I told my Mother about my experience, but she insisted that my new friend only resembled the girl in the casket. I heard my parents talking long into the night about the coincidence in names. I have always prayed for the dead after this experience.

I do not believe that Angelique was earthbound, but she needed help in accepting her death. When she appeared in my dream, she was asking me for assistance. When she disappeared after we prayed together, she had accepted her death. Angelique moved on to another dimension. Acceptance brings peace and release.

Have you ever have had an experience with a spirit? Have your friends ever shared a dream or an unusual experience with you? Sometimes it is best to write down meaningful dreams so that you can analyze them later. You may find that dreams can provide you with significant and valuable future information if you can understand the symbols that appear in your dreams.

## Dream Symbols can Predict the Future

I have talked above about common symbols and their possible interpretations. Sometimes symbols will appear in your dreams as future warnings or blessings. Study your dreams to understand the roles that symbols play in your everyday world. Get in touch with the inner you that is communicating with you symbolically. Find out what makes you tick. If you dream of a particular symbol, discover its meaning and apply its wisdom to your daily activities. If certain symbols appear repeatedly, they are significant messages from your subconscious. Your dreams are full of symbols from which you can benefit if you understand their messages and act on them.

Remember, most of your dreams are personal, so they will need to be interpreted according to your own perception and understanding. The significance of a dream symbol to one person may have a completely different meaning to another person. Symbols that appear in dreams can be important clues as to what is going on in your life now or in your future.

Sometimes your dreams do not beat around the bush. They are usually direct, but at other times your dream symbols, facial expressions, sounds, feelings, colors, and gestures must be put together like solving a murder mystery before you can successfully interpret your dreams.

## Dream Facial Features Can Predict Your Future

Faces are crucial to the expression of feelings and emotions. The characteristic parts of a person's face are the eyes, nose and mouth. The ability to read another person's facial expressions can predict the probability of subsequent behavior. A dream may speak in a symbolic language to emphasize just one of these external organs. For example, the eyes are the windows of the soul. Of course, the eyes are also considered symbols of perception, observation, watchfulness, protection, judgment, and prophecy to name just a few symbolic meanings.

Some dreams know how to grab your attention so it is not unusual to see an exaggerated facial feature, such as the eyes, to signal a red flag warning. If you dream of a person with gigantic eyes it may indicate a part of yourself that you are ignoring, failing to accept, look at, or simply let go. Before you go to SEE the optometrist, consider that a message featuring bizarre eyes can indicate where to look for problems in your real life that require your immediate attention.

Usually all parts of your dreams relate to you, including other exaggerated facial features such as the nose and mouth. Understated facial features or even missing body parts could indicate where you need to expand your point of view to see the bigger picture. When you experience major life changes, your strange dreams can signal these latest changes and will attempt to update you using symbols. Learn to connect your dreams with what is happening in your personal world. The following example will show you how to link dream symbols with your waking reality.

**Connie's Nose Gets Her in Trouble**

One night, Connie had a dream that really frightened her. In her dream, she could see herself gossiping to three co-workers about another absent woman. In real life, Connie was a nosey, snooping woman, and when she heard any new gossip she could hardly wait to tell the whole office. In her nightmare, Connie was amazed to feel her nose grow and grow as her captive audience listened to her latest gossip and stared in bewilderment. Connie was not telling lies like Pinocchio, but gossiping about other people's problems was mean and damaging. The dream was a definite warning to keep her nose out of other people's business or there could be serious consequences in the future.

Although Connie's nose was the exaggerated feature in her dream, her mouth should have costarred in the spotlight. Connie ignored the warning from her dream. Her obsession with workplace gossip eventually attracted employee discipline when malicious gossip began to cause problems between coworkers, and decrease teamwork productivity.

The moral of Connie's story is this: Before you consider gossiping, think twice to control your mouth and stop your nose from wandering off to sniff for trouble. You need to cut out gossiping in your thinking and in your words. Remember, if you dream of a gigantic nose or an enormous mouth, plastic surgery will not be the solution. Your perception of reality and understanding of these symbols will give meaning to your day-to-day life. Learn to connect your daily experience to your dreams for more in-depth meanings and solutions.

Have you ever experienced symbols in your dreams? What was going on with you at the time of your dreams? What were the symbols? Were they obvious or did you just recognize them after the fact? Think about shapes and objects. How did they speak to you? How did they make you feel?

Yes, the symbolic meaning of dreams should incorporate the overall feeling of the dream and the appearance of all noteworthy people in your everyday world. Some dreams contain no significant or recognizable people in the dream state but consist of a mixture of strangers and imaginary characters. If this is the case, look for symbols that may represent the missing people. Animals and birds also have important messages to give you regarding future events when they appear in your dreams. The following are two dream interpretations that involve symbols and animals.

### Maureen Gets a Promotion

In a vivid dream, Maureen saw herself sitting in the large, impressive office of her boss, Mr. Williams. There were thriving plants and beautiful photos hanging on the walls that captured her attention immediately. The energy of the office felt very good. Maureen felt comfortable and completely at ease. After a couple of minutes, her boss entered the office singing. He immediately smiled when he saw Maureen. On Mr. William's right shoulder sat a huge, talking parrot with brightly colored feathers and unclipped wings. Her boss easily silenced the parrot with a few *clucks* that the bird apparently understood and obeyed.

Mr. Williams then shook Maureen's hand with enthusiasm and happily handed her a large key on a red leather key chain. Maureen gladly accepted the key and walked out of the office with a song in her heart and a smile on her face. Maureen woke up feeling great! Three weeks later, Maureen received a large raise and a major promotion from Mr. Williams.

Remember, a key can lock or unlock. It can offer an ending or a new start. In this case, the key offered a new beginning.

### Jack Did Not Read the Warnings

Jack saw himself sitting nervously in the small, stale-smelling office of his manager, George. In the corner, on the floor, lay a small, dead gray mouse. The office itself appeared to be falling apart as Jack stared in amazement. If that were not enough to be concerned about, his boss's desk appeared to be slowly moving into a dark, spiraling tunnel.

Jack's boss suddenly appeared from the tunnel, pushing the escaping desk back into his office. The face of Jack's boss seemed to be drained of energy, and an unlit cigarette dangled from between his lips. Without greeting Jack, George handed him a key. Jack nervously accepted the key, but it disappeared and was immediately replaced with a lock.

At this point of the dream, Jack woke up sweating and feeling very uneasy. The next day at work, he noticed nothing suspicious, so he soon dismissed the nightmare from his mind. Jack was completely fooled by his physical senses. He did not question or look for red flags in his physical world that could have foretold coming work-related problems. Occasionally during the following days his dream flashed back into his mind, but he continued to disregard the forewarning. Two months later, Jack was called into his manager's office, where he was terminated without ceremony. He was told that the company was bankrupt and closing. Jack's reaction to the news was shock and disbelief. However, this should not have come as a surprise to Jack, considering what his subconscious was telling him.

## A Look at Both Dreams and Their Symbolism

Let's compare the two dreams to see what some of the symbols revealed. In Maureen's dream, the energy of the office felt good. The thriving plants and colorful pictures on the wall were symbols of light, energy, and life. Maureen felt very relaxed and at ease because she was centered and in control. After waiting a few more minutes, her boss entered the office singing and smiling. A large parrot with brightly colored feathers sat on Mr. Williams' right shoulder. Maureen noticed that the bird's wings were not clipped, so it was free to fly wherever it wished. The parrot had the ability to talk, but obediently remained silent when he was told to be quiet.

The power of the parrot to imitate sound, including human speech, is also suggestive of the subconscious to copy and reflect our own actions back to us. The parrot represented intelligence and the capability to listen, communicate, and duplicate. It symbolized Maureen's ability to change, adapt, balance, cooperate, and adjust to her new career position as a director working closely with her boss. Mr. Williams shook Maureen's hand and happily handed her a large key on a red leather key chain.

The colorful office, the talking parrot, the handshake, and the red key chain all symbolized life, activity, strength, and positive energy. Maureen gladly accepted the key and woke up feeling good. These were all good omens regarding her promotion. Her key opened doors and allowed her to move forward on the corporate ladder.

In the second dream, Jack waited in a small musty smelling office. There was a lack of permanence symbolized by the desk as it moved into the spiraling tunnel. The face of Jack's boss appeared to be drained of energy. George's unlit cigarette dangling from between his lips symbolized the lack of fire or enthusiasm that requires energy. Jack's boss represented the company. All were signs of a disappearing job, no money or energy, struggle, and death (of the company). The dead mouse was a symbolic of a done deal. The mouse also indicated Jack's inability to look at the bigger picture. Jack's boss did not smile or talk, but his demeanor spoke volumes. The dream was waving a red flag that something obvious was hidden from Jack's conscious mind. All of the symbolism pointed to negativity regarding Jack's future employment.

Jack's boss, George, merely shook his head slowly and silently handed Jack a key. These were all bad signs of limitations, obstacles, and restriction. If those were not strong enough messages, Jack should have gotten it when the key disappeared and was immediately replaced with a lock. At this point, Jack woke up from his nightmare sweating and feeling uneasy, a true gut-level warning.

When Jack was let go two months later, it should not have come as a surprise. Had he paid attention to his forewarning nightmare, he would have prepared for the death of his old company and now be working for another new employer. Death can also represent closure, release, and completion. If you look at Jack's dream from this perspective, Jack's termination could also be a new beginning and a blessing in disguise. After all, the end of Jack's old employment offered him future opportunities. All endings initiate new beginnings.

# CHAPTER EIGHTEEN NOTES

# CHAPTER NINETEEN
# Living in the Present Time

OUR FUTURE INVOLVES PHYSICAL TIME AND SPACE so time is of the essence when it comes to foreseeing upcoming events. Although hard facts cannot be received from the future, our strong emotional feelings about the future can flow backward in time to warn and guide us currently. We can pick up on premonitions about events yet to happen because our emotional inner-knowing is sensed through our subconscious as a strong gut-level feeling. Many of us have avoided a serious accident by paying attention to a powerful hunch, dream or vision that forewarned us.

Let's take a look at knowledge of the future from another point of view. This requires you to live in the present moment to pay attention to current situations. A change in your perception of life can definitely help you zero in on your future. A warning of things yet to come can almost always be seen as moving generally in a certain direction. Anything that the human mind sets in mental motion produces a physical consequence or effect. If you are paying attention to today, you will be able to foresee tomorrow, and, likewise, if you cannot live in the present moment, you will never be able to predict the coming future. What is your perception of time? Remember, wherever your consciousness is, you are. Being mentally somewhere else can make you constantly late and out of touch with reality.

## Your Perception of Time

Your perception of time can make you feel like a hopeless victim of circumstances. What is your perception of time? Your future could be immobilized by your own thinking. Your thoughts can freeze you in time and lock you in the twilight zone of *coulda, woulda, shoulda, remember when, if only,* and *someday.* These useless zombies rob you of living today as you try to relive the past that has already happened or to wait living in a "someday" world.

Every *if only* and *someday* thinking is really the unreleased hidden agents of regret, resentment, anger, hurt, procrastination, and wishful thinking. Someday thinking can give you a false sense of future security while controlling your choices and decisions. You should release such attitudes, or they will sabotage you forever today. It will be impossible to live if you continue to look at time from the eyes of the past or the eyes of the future. Keep your eyes on today because it is all that you have.

Procrastination is an enormous waste of time and energy and of your perceptions of control and reality. Procrastination is when you have so much faith in tomorrow that you take no action today. Appointments are forgotten or simply ignored. If you finally do remember your appointment, you try to catch up with a point in time that has already happened and is now the past. An uncertain, confused state of mind blames outside forces for the future and justifies its negative experiences with excuses and denials. Victims of life are unable to see the connection between their thinking and future physical experiences. If you are too bewildered to control today, it will be impossible to predict tomorrow.

The past, present, and future are intimately connected. Today was yesterday's future, and tomorrow will be today's past. It is in the present moment that you have the power to act and change the future. To get a glimpse of the future, pay close attention to your day-to-day experiences. How do you sense time? Does time crawl behind you like a snail or run past you like a cheetah? Where do you spend the majority of your mental time: in the past or in the future? When you play the "remember when" game, your thinking keeps you stuck, trying to live in a past that has already happened. That's impossible! If you play the future game of "someday," you put all of your energy into wishful thinking and the promise of tomorrow, and thus you cannot experience today. "Someday thinking" leads you to nothing but regrets and broken dreams.

You cannot live for the future in a "someday" world because it has not happened yet. If you live too much in the future, you will not be fully alive today. All of your future thinking will keep your happiness away from you today. Hoping and waiting for some future event takes your energy and consume today.

Do not wait until you get a major pay raise, your children leave home, you lose forty-five pounds, or you get a divorce to be happy. Enjoy life and be happy today because the present is all that you really have and can count on. Learn to accept your blessings day-to-day instead of waiting for the future that offers no guarantees. Shifting your focus from someday thinking to experiencing life today will definitely get to the core of your life's issues and help you understand and shape the future.

## Developing Presence

Your physical body is always present in this physical time frame, but where your thoughts and energy go, so go your focus and control. Out of body, out of mind! When you are talking with someone and your mind wanders, you become less competent to deal with your moment-to-moment reality. When your thoughts are scattered all over the place, so are you! The secret to developing presence is your ability to remain grounded. Your perception of life is determined by your ability to live in your moment-to-moment experiences. Certain moods keep you tuned out, not tuned in. For example, when you have a good day you see good everywhere, and when you have a bad day you focus just on the negative. If you keep in either mood, your thinking will pull in your thoughts in physical forms.

When your attention is on the past or future, you do things automatically and are not in touch with reality. Pay attention to how you feel throughout the day. If you feel lost, confused, angry, or uncertain, stop what you are doing and bring your attention back to this time and place. It is likely that you are reliving a past life experience, even if it happened an hour ago. To help you increase awareness and develop presence, sit in a comfortable place for a few minutes and relax. Keep your mind focused on the present moment. When you find yourself thinking in the past or future, bring your attention right back to the present moment. It is in the present time that you have the power to act and change your future. In fact, all that you have or will ever have is the present moment.

## CHAPTER NINETEEN NOTES

# CHAPTER TWENTY

# Your Profession and Common Sense

Today's overwhelming technological changes will require you to use common sense and stay in touch with your physical senses for reality checks. Actually, you will be forced to let go of some of your uncompromising beliefs, rethink your choices, and look at old habits that are influencing your personal life and your professional career.

Life is a non-stop journey around the Wheel of Life that requires future seeing to avoid psychological blind spots and head-on physical collisions. You must learn to anticipate the future while you still have options. Yes, moving up the corporate ladder will require you to look at the bigger picture, develop team spirit, and set common goals. Growth and mental transformation have their strong roots in change and your ability to adapt in order to survive on many levels. In your quest for self-understanding, this book allows a change in your perception of reality so that you are no longer controlled by the pattern of your old, predictable programming.

To increase your awareness and attention to detail, drive to work on a different route. You might wish to stick to the same old routine as it is convenient, but when you constantly engage in predetermined choices out of habit, boredom will set in and you will soon resort to thinking about the past or worrying about the future. Repetitious habits lead to preoccupation and fixation because they do not require your total attention. To wake up from your "automatic pilot" state of consciousness, choose a different route to go to work. You will be more aware because your attention will be challenged to remain in the present time. Do not wait for flashing red lights, ambulances, fire trucks, or police cars to get your full attention to predict your future.

## Enhance Your Perception at the Workplace

How do you perceive your work environment? Are your work habits predictable? When you get to your employment, where is your attention focused? What is the first thing that you do when you arrive at work? Do you head straight for the water cooler, coffee room, or restroom, or do you start up the computer and get ready to go to work?

What is your daily routine at your work environment? When you are on automatic pilot you miss corporate changes that may indicate future challenges that will affect your income or your employment status. If you are paying attention, you can make other arrangements before your future with the company is revealed with a pink termination notice or promotion.

Use your physical senses to stay in touch with your work surroundings. Your physical senses will provide you with the information you need to advance on the corporate ladder. Observe and listen to clues that will reveal coming times. Pay attention to the body language of your boss and coworkers. You will not be able to tune in if your mind is elsewhere fantasizing about getting a date with Suzy Q or the stud with the six-pack abs.

What is your perception of the people you work with on a daily basis? If you are disconnected by your own thoughts it will be difficult to put yourself in another person's position or read them. Your attitude will be clouded by your personal thoughts, which could be totally out of sync with your coworkers and prevent you from being a team player. You may be using your words constructively, but what is your body language revealing to the whole office or a particular coworker that is waiting to get your job? Unexpressed emotions can sting even if words are not heard.

Stop, look, and listen before you express your personal opinions in the office. Your boss or the boss's confidant could be standing right behind you. Listening, awareness, and observation will give you some control over your speech and body language. Remember, your words invoke powerful images, feelings, and unexpressed emotions that are felt even if they are not heard or seen. Your attitudes, words, thoughts, and feelings thrive where you live or work. Yes, even your gestures are mentally and emotionally recorded all around you, and later they are reproduced in your life as your future. At times your gut feelings speak much louder than your words. Your physical and instinctive impressions provide significant information when you trust in your feelings to guide you. If you keep in the present moment, intuition will kick in to reveal what you need to do to keep centered and in control.

If you look at your corporation from a detached perspective along with other co-workers, it will eventually affect your organization's ability to survive in the future. You will not see the simple connection that the corporation's success depends on productive employees who, in turn, depend on a paycheck from the company to survive. You must understand that everything depends on everything else to co-exist. If you cannot adapt to current personal and professional changes it will be more difficult to anticipate the future. When old strategies and actions no longer work, it is time to include mental and spiritual laws for your personal and future professional success. Positive change and the power of intuition can increase your professional excellence on levels that you never dreamed were possible. This expansion of your mind will increase your professional viewpoint from just "doing a job" to being a productive team player. Hopefully, it will increase your income as well.

**Practice Self-Observation**
Do not fool yourself: even the least intelligent people in the office can telepathically pick up on your intentions and feelings toward them. Discipline and monitor your thoughts, and you can change your behavior, and this can change your work opportunities. Make a conscious effort to change your attitude today to ensure your employment tomorrow. Do not leave things to chance or luck. The following information will help you with your decision making and things that can take you out of the present moment.

Pay attention to your physical environment constantly. What do your physical senses tell you about the present time? When you get anxious and stressed about the future, simply disconnect from the future. Practice meditating to withdraw from the distractions of everyday living for a few minutes once a day. Put yourself in the sanctuary of your own mind to heal and promote mental wellness. As you make progress, you may increase the amount of time you spend disconnecting. Use the following questions to help you remain in the present time.

## Present Moment Questions
1. What am I thinking now?
2. How am I feeling?
3. Is any part of my body feeling pain or tension?
4. Is there a person, a place, or a thing that I need to release?
5. Am I living in the present moment, or am I living in the past or future?

## Simple Decision-Making Tools
At times, you may fail to make decisions because you are uncertain and do not know what to decide on. When you are unsure of what you want out of life, you procrastinate about decision making because you are immobilized by your uncertainties. The Wheel of Life constantly turns but requires movement to make progress. Life expects us to face challenges and adapt to changing circumstances. Each season of life offers new beginnings, changes, blessings, and hope for the future. The Wheel of Life also brings closures, completions, loss, and pain. Remember, all endings also offer something new to anticipate. The ability to recognize a time for closure and letting go is an important process that tells the subconscious that we are ready to move forward.

The majority of your negative experiences indicate where change is necessary. They offer you opportunities to initiate decisions and face challenges. When there are too many options, it is difficult to make decisions, and so you may leave your future to chance or fate. Occasionally, too many possible choices lead to your making no decision.

Decisions can be made when you look at your options objectively and from several different angles. You must separate the advantages and disadvantages of a situation on paper. What are the arguments for and against something? Do not generalize; be very specific, simple, and direct.

When you debate all the pros and cons of an issue, come to a final conclusion and act on it. Do not keep going back and forth once you make up your mind. Most people do not know when to stop asking questions or do not listen to the answers. I once talked to a very intelligent lady for over two hours in an intuitive life coaching session. I provided her with answers to all of her questions. When our session was complete, I walked Margie to the front door. She turned around to thank me again, and then she said, "Now, what should I do again?"

Learn to listen and pay attention to answers. Decision making requires conscious choices, good questions, and good listening skills. Your decisions are not fixed in time. You can change your mind. Do not refuse to consider other options when you come to a dead end in your thinking.

Your decisions are constantly subject to change, yet most of your choices are predictable because of habit. Decisions can be inspired, modified, and altered by persuasion. Can you be persuaded to change your mind? Are you easily swayed by the opinions of other people? An appeal to your conscious mind can redirect your thinking into almost any direction, as most controlling individuals know.

Think clearly before you make a final decision. When you respond automatically to a situation, you give up your freedom to consider other options. You always have choices, so think of the likely consequences of your decisions. Who or what will your decision affect? After considering possibilities, work on individual issues. Remember, there is a price to pay for every decision or choice you make. Make sure that the decisions you make are for your highest good.

You will be in a better position to make decisions if you think things through before you act on your choices. Your gut feeling can be a reliable source of information that is automatically accessible when you integrate your common sense with decision-making.

Here are four simple questions to ask yourself before making decisions. Make sure to be in touch with your feelings and ask yourself the following questions.

## Simple Decision-Making Questions

1. What do I want?
2. What will it cost me?
3. Can I afford it?
4. Is it worth it?

## Lack of Attention and Accidents

Lack of attention and stress are significantly related to traffic accidents. Before you blame the other driver, make it a point to discern if the accident could have been avoided by you. When people have a lot of problems, they become preoccupied with their concerns and do not pay attention to what they are doing. During periods of stress in your life, your odds of getting in an accident greatly increase. Accidents can be predicted because people under pressure make mistakes in judgments. When your mind is preoccupied with a problem that is where your focus lies. People not paying attention to what they are doing cause the most accidents.

You mind is focused on where your emotions live. Cell phones and driving do not mix. Drivers using cell phones are more likely to get into a serious car crash. When you get involved in emotional conversations on your cell phone, you forget that you are behind the wheel. Many people in a variety of situations have accidents because they are preoccupied with their own thoughts. Your ancestors lived in nature and paid close attention to their environment. A lack of attention in ancient times could mean being an instant take-out dinner for a wild animal waiting for a distracted victim. Instinct and the desire to survive kept your ancestors alert and aware of their physical world.

Accidents are messages to pay attention to what you are doing. How many times have your personal problems interfered with your driving ability? Have you ever missed an exit because you were lost in your own thoughts? Mistakes are made when your physical body is in one place and your mind is elsewhere. Driving a motor vehicle demands your full attention. You must remain awake and alert if you are to avoid accidents and possible death in the future.

# CHAPTER TWENTY NOTES

# CHAPTER TWENTY-ONE

# The Power of Affirmations

C HANGE REQUIRES THAT YOU ADAPT to new situations, persons, places, and things. If you cannot adjust quickly, stress and frustration enter your life, taking away your control and power to see the future. When you are in a stressful situation, you must stop your mind from reacting according to past programming. A walk down Memory Lane may not be what you had in mind when you find yourself on a road that leads to nowhere but frustration.

You can create affirmations to improve the quality of your personal and professional goals and objectives. The powers of affirmations are their suggestive value. Words and thoughts keep you on track for what you are trying to accomplish. However, you cannot say one thing and think something else, or you will get what you have subconsciously prepared yourself for. Using positive verbal trigger words, such as those in affirmations, can provide you with an instant attitude adjustment. Silently repeating an affirmation can redirect your mind toward an optimistic outcome. You can use specific words to control your emotions, shut out negative self-talk, change an outcome, and reprogram your future. Focused control and direction replace random thoughts with specific goals and the intention to change the future.

When you catch yourself getting emotionally out of control, you can consciously take back your power by simply stating, "I will not go there." In other words, "I will not allow myself to continue unproductive behavior out of habit. I will not allow my old thinking patterns to kick me to the curb."

When you find yourself caught up in the past, in a "coulda, woulda, shoulda" mood, use the command, "Stop it!" for an instant attitude adjustment to move your thoughts beyond past programming. When dealing with procrastination, here is an effective statement to help you eliminate postponement: "Now is the time to begin and complete projects and goals." Repeat your preferred affirmations as many times as necessary. Focus on what you want to achieve, and your intuition will follow with a flash of insight. You know what you need to work on to change the future.

You may even want to develop your own rituals for focusing on positive affirmations. For example, you could look into the mirror in the morning and say the statements you have selected to help shape your outlook for the day. You may add your own affirmations to this list. Choose a few affirmations from the following list of examples to help you change past programming.

## Affirmations: The Power of Auto-Suggestions

### For self-direction and developing self-trust:
1. I now effectively control my life. I accept responsibility for my choices.
2. I direct my thoughts and actions toward accomplishing my goals.
3. I make right choices and decisions for my Highest Good. I trust myself.
4. I consciously control my destiny by releasing all false self-fulfilling prophecies.
5. I attract good things to me easily and successfully.

### For self-help and personal empowerment:
1. The good that I seek is also seeking me.
2. I treat people with compassion, kindness, and respect.
3. I am loyal, understanding, and just.
4. I am a good person, and I attract the right conditions in all of my affairs.
5. I put closure on the past. I am open to change and new beginnings.

**For emotional release and positive relationships:**
1. I release and let go of whoever is not for my highest good.
2. I consciously let go of whatever is irritating me or making me sick.
3. I am thankful for all my blessings and the blessings of other people.
4. I now consciously let go of procrastination, worry, and anxiety.
5. I let go of doubt and uncertainty. I now experience faith and trust.

**For awareness of the present:**
1. I live in the moment and in a conscious state of awareness.
2. I make conscious choices and decisions. I am no longer limited by past choices.
3. I am open to new ideas, new options, and possibilities.
4. I constantly rise above self-imposed limitations.
5. I take good care of my body with the proper amount of food, rest, and exercise.

**For dealing with daily life:**
1. I manage my time at work and at home productively.
2. I listen to my intuition for guidance, instruction, and healing.
3. I get excellent financial compensation for providing excellent service.
4. I am a spiritual being. The physical boundaries of time and space do not limit me.
5. The wise person within me speaks, and I listen and learn.

**For acceptance of self, others, and the world:**
1. I love and respect myself. I forgive myself and other people for past mistakes.
2. I respect nature and the environment. I do my part to preserve its resources.
3. I am now free of old negative habits and past programming
4. I respect the rights of other people's opinions and property.
5. I am considerate of my neighbors. I realize that my neighbors live all over the world.

# CHAPTER TWENTY-ONE NOTES

CHAPTER TWENTY-TWO

# The Universal Law of Cause and Effect

YOU MAY BE MORE FAMILIAR with the Universal Law of Cause and Effect as exemplified by the concept of karma, often expressed as "what goes around comes around." All of your physical experiences are created by your subconscious through the law of cause and effect, which are mental actions and physical reactions. You first make things happen in your mind with your original thoughts. Then you experience those thoughts as they are manifested in your life experiences. These experiences are the effects of your choices. Lack of knowledge of the law of cause and effect does not exempt you from its mode of action. If you pay attention and observe your daily experiences, you will eventually connect them with your thinking. An awareness of this phenomenon will empower you to shape your future

When you prepare for the future you are able to control certain outcomes as preventive measures. When you understand cause and effect, you recognize how the inner dynamics of your thoughts, choices, and actions are revealed in the outcome of your future experiences. The Universal Law of Cause and Effect can be compared to what is often called the domino effect. The consequence of one event setting off a chain reaction of similar events can result from seemingly minor actions that can cause major elements of life to spiral out of control. The subconscious completely depends on the conscious mind for its direction and guidance. The physical senses tell it what is out there in the physical world. Its job is to help you act from the information that you give it, most importantly for survival.

When the conscious mind makes the wrong choice, there is sometimes an immediate effect. For example, a mother might warn her young son not to touch the hot teapot. When the mother turns around to reach for the sugar, the boy touches the hot pot and is burned. Pain is the immediate consequence of the act itself. The child is not punished by some outside force for disobeying his mother. The choice of touching the hot teapot is the cause, and the automatic pain is the effect or result of that outcome. Every choice or action has a consequence, and everything that you see or feel in the physical world is an effect, not a cause. In other words, your physical reality is the outcome of your thinking and choices.

In your subconscious are the tendencies or mental seeds of the future that can be changed today if you are paying attention. Remember, your thoughts shape your destiny, so the best way to prepare for the future is to live in the present time constructively. Your fixed day-to-day attitude creates specific conditions that determine a lot of things in your life. You can no longer blame someone else for your problems or circumstances. If you refuse to take responsibility for your life, you will become a helpless victim of conditions.

As I have stated throughout this book, sooner or later we all experience unexpected occurrences out of the blue. This is not fate; neither does it imply that your future is prearranged by other forces. While you cannot control all of your life experiences, some of your future is controllable because it is not fixed in time. The past has already happened, so it is fixed. There is absolutely nothing you can do today to change the past. However, some of the future is changeable because it has not happened as yet. Do you still believe that your future is fixed in time or predetermined by external forces? What about your choices and free will? Who or what is controlling your life or destiny? If the future is indeed prearranged, then you have no free will, no choices, and no accountability. But no, we are all born with free will within a given context of circumstances and a potential that includes a blueprint of possibilities.

## Things to Think About

Your subconscious is the law of your life. This is one of the most important concepts I want you to understand. Are you ready to listen with your heart, by which I mean the subconscious, and your conscious mind? Initially you may feel resentment and anger at the following statements. But the good news is that when your psychological blind spots are removed your perception expands. This allows you to recognize the truth because you can now see the cause of some of your problems. The subsequent statements should actually make you feel relieved. If not, you may still be fooled by only looking at your outside circumstances (effects). Instead, you must look within to determine the source of your troubles. Keep in mind that you must apply any new knowledge before it actually becomes wisdom. Remember, God does not get even, but the Universal Law of Cause and Effect does. Allow the following words to sink in before you react defensively.

- God does not punish you, curse you, or bestow favoritism.
- It is not God's will to make you suffer, grieve, or have limited funds.
- God does not give you bad relationships or heartaches, but your own choices do.
- Do not blame God for your pain, accidents, losses, illnesses, or failures,
- Do not blame God for your negative self-fulfilling prophecies, bad luck, or fate.
- When a loved one makes bad choices, do not blame God for their mistakes.
- God doesn't make you pay for repeated mistakes, but your own decisions produce certain outcomes.

It is the law of cause and effect in your own subconscious that settles the scores on your mistaken thinking and choices, not God. *Retribution is mine; I will repay,* says the Universal Law of Cause and Effect. This law results in automatic payback without judgment or prejudice. Every action or choice that you make has an automatic reaction or consequence. The Bible suggests the Universal Law of Cause and Effect with these words: "As you sow, so shall ye reap." In other words, the seeds you plant today in the soil of your subconscious you will reap in your physical world tomorrow as effects. Other instances of the law of cause and effect in the

Bible include, "It is done unto you as you believe," "An eye for an eye and a tooth for a tooth," and "They have sown the wind, and they will reap the whirlwind." No beating around the bush in these biblical statements!

These powerful words from the Bible and other significant sacred books of Buddhism and Hinduism indicate that you cannot evade the Universal Law of Cause and Effect because it is a natural part of you. There is automatic justice without judgment, and that means there is no such thing as a cause without an effect. The effects that you see in your outside physical world are of the same nature as the cause that created them. It is impossible to think one thing and produce something else. Automatic justice without judgment or prejudice makes sense because it is the truth.

Meditation, prayers, and affirmations free us from old programming that is producing the same old outcomes repeatedly. In order to initiate change, we must get at the original root cause of the outcomes we experience from the choices we make. If we get to the cause of why something happens to us, we can also determine the effect or outcome. Remember, your destiny is not controlled by outside forces. Your destiny is the result of cause and effect. Perhaps this gives us all something to think about as we learn to link our choices (cause) to our outside experiences (effect).

## CHAPTER TWENTY-TWO NOTES

## CHAPTER TWENTY-THREE
# Uniting Intuition and Feelings with Logic

INTUITION IS EMOTIONAL INTELLIGENCE so can it be successfully united with feelings and logic? The answer is yes! Intuition connects with your gut-level feelings and conscious mind. It is a vital part of your intellect and determines your courses of action. If you take the time to think before you make important decisions, intuition and instinct join together as a beneficial part of your decision-making process. Intuition is *most effective* when the logical conscious mind thinks, questions, and plans toward a specific objective or goal. When the conscious mind is educated on a particular topic, intuition steps in to provide information that was previously inaccessible. The conscious mind then recognizes mental tendencies *already set in motion* to draw its answers and come to a final conclusion.

Your conscious mind works best with your deliberate thought process to get answers and solutions. Ask the right question, and you will get the right answer. An uncertain and confused mind can only produce puzzled indecision. It is very helpful to write your question and see if you can get a sense of the answer. How does your question feel? If you fear a particular outcome it will influence your ability to get an answer. Get in touch with your feelings, and your physical body will communicate with you.

To get something you have to give something. In this case, you are giving your question and anticipating an answer to something that wants to answer you. Relax, and your answer will come to you from a person, place, or thing. If you are asking, but feel you are not receiving answers, perhaps you just do not recognize the form the answers take when the response is received. Do not keep asking the same question over and over. Give your subconscious time to respond to your request. Your answer can be influenced by the power of suggestion to your own subconscious. Your fears can easily jam up the communication link with doubt and negative mental chatter.

Instinct draws its knowledge from the subconscious. This part of the mind is common to all of us. It is not just personal; it is *trained* by your past experiences to respond in a particular manner. Intuition, in comparison, integrates from both your personal life experiences and your subconscious, gut-level feelings. Intuition is a higher level of your own consciousness. It is another aspect of you, and is sometimes referred to as your Higher-Self or your Inner-Self. It is a part of the divine, universal, sustaining source of all guidance and wisdom. It offers you a strong sense of well-being, and it opens a treasure chest of possibilities, answers, and opportunities to you.

Your physical emotions shout at you for attention, so they can easily distract you from the quiet voice of intuition, which is sometimes vague and difficult to define when you are not paying attention. When evaluating intuition, use common sense and remember that intuition does not control, shout, fight, argue, command, or destroy. This book will definitely give you another perspective to look at your world so that you can intuitively recognize what your sixth sense is revealing.

Intuition expands your awareness beyond the physical boundaries of your habits and the gut-level feeling of the emotional knowing of the physical body that is instinct. Intuition is an inner awareness with direct freedom to access information independent of any reasoning or logical course of action. Intuition is inner-knowing that gives you a direct understanding of reality without the siren of your gut feelings. It is accurate and unfailing in its ability to uplift, inspire, heal, guide, protect, and advise you.

The inner knowing of intuition gives you an immediate understanding of reality despite the logical mind's need for proof and the hard, cold facts of the conscious mind. The nature of intuition is understanding, loving, focused, healing, creative, and original. Intuition opens a world of possibilities, answers, creativity, solutions, and opportunities as they present themselves.

Intuition can integrate with instinct as a physical sensation and may take the form of images, strong urges, ideas, feelings, symbols, words, inspiration, déjà vu, and simple knowing. Dreams, visions, hunches, omens, telepathy, and synchronicity bypass reason and logic by giving you an intuitive understanding of things yet to come, if you pay attention.

Intuition deals with feelings that must be translated into words. Impressions enter the mind in a flash and are gone before you know it. Feelings linger and must be interpreted by the conscious mind. Intuition can provide instant understanding without the benefit of the reasoning mind. An impression is a form of feeling that could be bad or good depending on its suggestive value. Impressions are flashes of information, insight, ideas, facts, and images that leap from the subconscious into the conscious mind. Intuition then steps in with immediate knowledge and understanding to capture the moment. You must either flash forward or fall behind.

A hunch, that strong desire to do something that cannot be validated at the time, should never be ignored. Your intuition always tries to help you solve your problems and challenges. It is your responsibility to judge if it is a true impression or not. You must put aside your apprehensions and fears, or they will interfere with incoming intuitive impressions. Training your mind to pay attention will help you enhance sensory awareness and encourage intuitive functioning. How reliable is your intuition? How much should you depend on your gut-level feelings rather than on your rational mind? Observance, trust, faith, expectation, and application will determine the validly of your intuition.

# CHAPTER TWENTY-THREE NOTES

# CHAPTER TWENTY-FOUR

# A Flash Forward Plan to Shape Your Future

YOU ARE ON A LIFELONG JOURNEY on the Wheel of Life that requires constant movement and change. Do not wait for a someday world of wishful thinking to get you rolling. You may not always know what the future holds, but planning and preparing for it offers valuable direction and some control over outcomes. Most people do not recognize goal setting as a tool to help create their future. Goals help you to take charge of your life and initiate change. Having goals will allow you to make conscious lifestyle choices and take actions to shape your future today.

Don't drift through life without a destination in mind. Living life without goals is like trying to drive a car without an engine or trying to float a boat without a sail. Goal setting is a roadmap to help you reach your upcoming destination. Today is a brand new beginning. It offers you fresh opportunities and unlimited potential. Do not get stuck in a rut by reminiscing about your past accomplishments. If you spend too much time looking back, you will be unable to move forward today. Goals offer a sense of direction and an awareness of something new to anticipate.

Goal setting allows you to make decisions about your own future. Goals also help you reprogram old thinking patterns to change the future. Keep moving in your minds, my friends! What does your future hold in your mind's eye?

## Daydreaming and Visualization

Einstein, one of the greatest scientists the world has ever produced, confessed that he spent much of his life daydreaming. He later explained that he came to understand this daydreaming habit as his way of conducting "thought experiments" in which he projected ideas and engaged in their possible scientific implications. He experienced daydreaming as a way to free up his mind from inhibiting rules and regulations to explore creative thinking as a prelude to action in the practical world of reality.

You don't have to be Einstein to justify daydreaming. Daydreaming can move you beyond the wishful thinking and struggling for answers of the conscious mind. The power of daydreams is linked to the creative power of the subconscious. Anything that you visualize or think about long enough can become your reality. Daydreaming can provide inspiration to improve your performance in life, your ability to express yourself creatively, your capacity to experience physical and mental health, and other important objectives.

Coaches and teachers encourage athletes, students, and performing artists to use the power of visualization to shape their future to achieve outstanding accomplishments. They vividly imagine experiencing success, improving acting skills, achieving a victory, or winning an important race to reach their goals and achieve medal-winning performances. Tiger Woods uses visualization or daydreams to keep him on the top of his golf game. When you visually impress your subconscious with your objectives, it will automatically move you toward your goals. Developing a strong vision of a future goal will definitely help you accomplish it. Yes, your imagination can be trained to produce rich sensory images to help you help yourself to realize your goals.

Anything that you visualize or think about long enough can serve to shape your future and become your reality. Visualizing success helps everyone perform better mentally, emotionally, and physically. Use your physical senses to make your goals real. If you can see the future clearly in your mind's eye, you can produce it in your physical world. Today, see your future as you want it to unfold tomorrow. The future exists as potential, determined by causes that bring events to pass. Planning ahead is like *planting* ahead. Like the farmer, you decide on the seeds for the harvest you desire. However, all seeds in a garden require care and maintenance. There are certain things that you must do to produce a healthy harvest, such as keeping the garden weeded, watered, and fed.

You cannot make a goal and expect it to produce your expectations without any work on your part. What do you do to keep motivated to work toward realizing your goals? What energy and time do you contribute to your goals? Goal-setting, self-study, preparation, and conscious choices will reveal opportunities to alter your future as you prepare for coming times. When life waves red flags, it is time to make changes and set new goals. No matter what your challenges are, you can bring yourself into unity with constructive inner forces to celebrate life masterfully, solve problems, and attain your goals.

Intuition and gut-level feelings also play important roles in determining the outcome of future goals. Pay attention to strong feelings, dreams, and omens from nature regarding your goals. A dream may communicate with you through a symbolic message to help you achieve a particular goal. An irritating fly may warn you that it is bad timing to ask your boss for a raise when he is already irritated with your job performance. Your goal would be to improve your job performance before requesting an increase in your paycheck. Seeing two dogs fighting in the street may indicate that it is best to avoid a confrontation with a driver that cuts you off on the freeway. Your goal would definitely be to abide by the symbolic message you received and ignore annoyances that could result in destructive confrontations.

Yes, the universe is full of personal messages to help you avoid problems. Your sixth sense can help you apply common sense toward defining and realizing goals that are right for you in relationship to the context of your situation. Pay attention to daily messages as they are revealed. As you can see, we all have goals even if the primary goal is only to live another day. To get into the flow of good physical and mental health you need to manage your time and energy for better performance. Watch your personal habits to reduce stress levels and self-sabotage. Be aware of negative self-talk and beliefs that can block the attainment of your goals. Unresolved issues can affect your productivity and lead to anger, depression, and low energy levels.

Take time to disconnect from distracting influences on a regular basis. Learn to relax and get the proper food and sleep to boost your energy levels and concentration. A healthy body and mind can keep you spiritually strong and improve your work performance. Missing too many work days because of illness or poor planning is a fast way to get terminated.

Goals help you focus, plan, prepare, address specific needs, and produce change in accordance with your objectives. Successful people never play it by ear or trust in chance alone. They map out their destiny in advance with a written plan of action to eliminate chance and uncertainty. The purpose of setting goals in writing is to create a specific plan to direct your mind and clarify your ideas and objectives. Knowing exactly what you want out of life can make your wildest dreams come true. You need to construct a specific plan of action if you are to achieve your goals without getting sidetracked by procrastination and the zombies of regret and someday thinking. Your heart's desires may hint at possible goals and a sense of direction. If your heart (subconscious) is not into your goal, the conscious mind cannot produce it.

**Create a to-do List**

Your future is created by your moment-to-moment choices and decisions. Your intentions and focus will determine your success or failure with your goals. In addition to goal setting, you can create a daily to-do list to help you organize your time and prioritize your tasks. A to-do list is a helpful way to stay on track with your goals. This will help you avoid procrastination and mental blocks that keep you limited and afraid of the future. It will help you increase your efficiency, memory, and decision-making skills. Another benefit is managing your time more productively. Your goals must be specific and clear, and so must your to-do list. You can put your most important task at the top of the list and your less important task at the bottom. Cross off your tasks as you complete them and continue to update your to-do list as needed. Your to-do list can successfully work with your goal-setting plan as a team to help you make productive choices.

To be effective, goals should have a time frame or they will be only wishful thinking. Setting goals requires making the appropriate decisions today. The inability to make choices and decisions leads to procrastination and dead dreams. Goals help you take charge of your life and control the future to a greater extent. After nearly fifty years as an intuitive specialist and holistic life coach, it is clear to me that you must plan, prepare, and take actions toward your objectives to shape your future. You cannot afford to leave your destiny to chance or fate. Some people believe that *fate* is a predetermined succession of events that are inevitable or unavoidable. *Fate* implies no choices and no control over one's own future. But I believe that you can create the succession of events that you want to experience in your future. You do this when you set goals, pay attention to current conditions, take action, and are willing to adapt to changes. Your destiny involves change, action, and movement. This is what goal setting is all about.

Okay, let's start choosing the seeds that you want to plant today so you can harvest the crop you want tomorrow. The following steps will help you plan, prepare, and take action in goal-setting today for the future.

## A Flash Forward Plan to Accomplish your Goals

**Step 1. Flash Forward: Determine your future goals.** List what you want to accomplish or attain in the future. Be specific about what you are trying to achieve. What does your heart want you to do? What are your intuition and gut-level feelings telling you about your goals? What is your mind telling you about your objectives? Keep in touch with your inner self. Write your goals as clearly as possible. Do not limit your hopes, expectations and ideas. Trust in your intuition and do not be afraid to stalk your dreams. Plan BIG! Anything is possible if you believe.

_____

_____

_____

_____

_____

_____

**Step 2. Flash Forward: Create an elimination list.** Most of your roadblocks are mental obstacles and self-imposed limitations. Make a list of persons, places, and things that are possible threats to your success. You already know who or what they are. Be careful of self-sabotage. Don't blame lack of education, poor communication, and bad social skills on fate or other people. Develop your listening skills, team spirit, and cooperation on a daily basis. Keep up to date in your area of expertise. Let go of your past failures, regrets, and resentments. What are some of your fears, feelings, and concerns regarding your future goals? What things do you need to release? Write them down.

_____

_____

_____

_____

_____

_____

**Step 3. Flash Forward: List strategies to achieve your goals.** You need a strong specific action plan to achieve your objectives and anticipate your future. Do not procrastinate, make excuses, or keep changing your mind about your goals. Changing a habit, losing ten pounds, or setting goals will require patience, motivation and commitment. Don't allow old habits to sneak in and sabotage you. Eliminate self-defeating thoughts and behaviors that are counter-productive. If you are trying to lose weight, do not keep candy and cookies in the house or in the office. Get rid of temptations. The same is true if you are trying to break old behavior patterns in any other areas of your life.

_____

_____

_____

_____

_____

_____

**Step 4. Flash Forward: Set a future target date.** Do not take on too many projects that can interfere with attaining your goals or completing them. Break up your goals into three manageable timeframes that you can handle without getting burned out. List your short-term goals, intermediate goals, and long-term goals. Be sure that your daily activities include a to-do list to create specific movement toward your objectives. Review your goals daily as a reminder to take action. Your future is in your own hands and your potential exists in your own mind as a miracle waiting to happen.

**List short-term goals (one week to a month)**

_____

_____

_____

**List intermediate goals (three to six months)**

_____

_____

_____

**List long-term goals (six months to a year)**

_____

_____

_____

**Step 5. Flash Forward: Prioritize your future goals.** Decide on your most important goals. Try not to work on too many goals at one time. It is better to accomplish a few goals than not complete any of them. Number your short, intermediate, and long-term goals according to priority and importance. Keep it simple! Think carefully, then list goals here on a scale from 1-3. Put a 3 beside the least important of your goals. For a top priority goal, put a 1. If you have more goals, add more numbers, but don't get carried away with just writing your goals. To achieve success you must take action steps as well.

_____

_____

_____

_____

**Step 6. Flash Forward: Anticipate future benefits.** Can you anticipate a work promotion, a pay raise or other fringe benefits you can expect upon achievement of your goals? Will you receive career recognition or be able to purchase a new home, a get-away cabin in the mountains, or perhaps that brand new Corvette that you have been eyeing? Motivation is the engine of incentive that moves you to the top of your profession. Write down what you can anticipate. Go for it!

_____

_____

_____

_____

_____

_____

**Step 7. Flash Forward: Start a plan of action today.** Do not procrastinate or make excuses and denials. Take responsibility for your life and your day-to-day choices. Remind yourself of your goals and pay attention to unexpected opportunities. Listen to what the universe has to tell you regarding your goals. Every day make a progress report to keep you on track. This will tell your subconscious that you are serious. Be aware that your daily choices and decisions will affect the outcome of your goals. Create a collage of your objectives in the form of pictures, symbols, and affirmations. Visualize the attainment of your goals in your mind's eye. The potential is within you, but you must make it happen!

_____

_____

_____

_____

_____

_____

**Step 8. Flash Forward: Celebrate goal accomplishments.** Congratulations! At last, the future has arrived and it's just what you expected! Wow! It is time to celebrate your achievements! You deserve a celebration! Mark each goal by writing the date of your accomplishment and the benefits of having accomplished that goal. You succeeded because you set goals and took action to achieve them. Your goals were not accomplished by chance or fate! Review your accomplishments on a regular basis to strengthen your confidence and shape your future just the way that you want to experience it.

The date of accomplishment: _____

Fringe Benefits: _____

The date of accomplishment: _____

Fringe Benefits: _____

The date of accomplishment: _____

Fringe Benefits: _____

**Step 9. Flash Forward: Time to set new goals.** Do not wait too long before setting new goals. Time is of the essence. The clock is ticking and time is moving forward. Time brings many changes into your life so you must learn to be flexible. Sometimes you must adapt your goals to changing times. You may need to redefine an old goal or let it go. Do not sit back and wait for your future to happen without your active participation. Flash forward into your future today. If you want to soar with the eagles, your goals will help you fly high above the storms of life right into the clear skies of tomorrow.

_____

_____

_____

_____

_____

_____

**Step 10. Flash forward: Bless your goals!** Don't forget to be thankful for your accomplishments, dreams, prosperity, ideas, employment, health, relationships and other blessings. Be a team player! Success happens when you bless yourself and everyone else you encounter on the Wheel of Life. *Now* is the time to start planning and preparing for your future goals with the confidence and peace of mind that can only come from taking command of your life. Exercise courage and become the victorious captain of your own ship. Otherwise you may become a boat-less victim adrift at sea, helplessly facing the wild winds of fate. The choice is yours. Your future is YOUR future. Writing down a goal is the first step toward making a dream come true. Now is the time to launch your ship of dreams.

## CHAPTER TWENTY-FOUR NOTES

# CHAPTER TWENTY-FIVE
# Expanding Your Perception of Spirit

THIS BOOK CELEBRATES our diversity and acknowledges a Universal Spirit that unites us all regardless of our outside physical differences. It is the unquestionable link to inner-knowing. Not all of your knowledge is obtained from your physical senses and the tangible world. Some of your knowledge is acquired intuitively without the logical, reasoning mind. When subconscious instinct and intuition integrate as one, they are capable of sensing future events, conditions, and situations before the conscious mind is aware of them. This means that you can give and receive information about the future intuitively because it is the natural link to your inner-knowing.

There is a primal Universal Spiritual Power that all things share. It is an essential part of our existence because it exists everywhere as a sea of energy in and around everything. This includes the seen material world and the unseen mental world of thought and spirit. This Universal Spirit responds to our emotional needs, connecting us to each other and to nature with its amazing array of plants, minerals, and animals.

The consciousness of Spirit lives in the animals, plants, rocks, mountains, oceans, and in us; what is collectively called the Great Spirit. To expand your perception of Spirit you must understand that you see the Great Spirit every time you observe a majestic mountain, a towering tree, a winding river, a magnificent sunrise, a shinning star, and a breathtaking sunset. You hear the voice of Spirit every time you listen to the birds sing, the winds blow, the laugher of a child, the sound of falling rain, and the cry of the eagle. All is the voice and eyes of Spirit.

Most people understand this Spiritual Power from their particular perspective and subjective experience. You recognize reality according to your belief system, religion, culture, symbols, and personal point of view. For that reason, the Universal Spirit has been acknowledged by many people across time and across cultures. It is called many names, such as the Great Spirit, the Holy Spirit, the Universal Spirit, the Universal Mind, the Universal Consciousness, the Creator, and, of course, God. Whatever name you choose to call this Infinite Spirit, it exists within everyone and everything as a natural resource of all wisdom and knowledge. It is a vital part of your consciousness and it is individualized by each of you through your separate and distinct personality.

Your ability to reach deeply within this essence of life to tap its spiritual power is determined by your capability to let go of limiting beliefs, negative emotions, and mistaken concepts that can become habitual, leaving you trapped and unproductive. You can easily become a prisoner by your own past programming. Your interpretation of any situation is influenced by your past experiences and present state of mind. To change your level of perception you can learn to move your consciousness to other levels that you are already plugged into for knowledge, guidance, healing, protection, and inner-knowing.

Tap the realm of this miracle-working essential source for answers and solutions. Your own inner resources offer unlimited potential for the birth of new ideas and new ways of directing your mind toward shaping your future in positive ways. Believing in miracles is what makes them happen. But we must also believe that we deserve to be blessed with miracles. The ability to perceive and receive our blessings is our natural birthright.

Flashing forward really requires flashing inward to integrate the physical, emotional, intellectual, intuitive, and spiritual dimensions of our human experience. Even the environment and the realm of nature must be considered. Despite our technological and scientific progress as a species, we cannot ignore the fact that we are members of the earth family that includes all living things on our planet. Recognizing that this ancient heritage is still a part of our modern identity reinforces the strong linkage of our collective perspective to our individual power of intuition.

You must remember, there is much more to life than what you perceive through your physical senses. The never-ending potential of the human mind offers a level of consciousness that has no time limits, no boundaries and no limitations. When your awareness is turned inward, the door to intuition opens you to direct revelations, experiences, and some events that cannot be explained or attributed to ordinary or coincidental occurrences.

You must be careful not to let technology and other distractions cause you to discount the power of your humanity, your faith, your intuition, and your common sense. Technology can repress your intuitive sense, but human spirituality and mental transformation require us to responsibly integrate feelings and observation of omens with intuition and logic.

Let us move beyond the limitations of our past perceptions and develop the strength to meet the challenges of changing times together. As we reach new levels of understanding we can expand our perception of the Universal Spirit and our connection with everything in our environment. When intuition is abandoned to the power of intellect alone, we cut off a critical portion of our natural heritage and block out a magnificent glimpse of our foreseeable future.

Remember, a lot of the future is shapeable so it's not too late to change your destiny. Don't leave your future to chance or fate. Learn to control your destiny to a greater degree. Move beyond self-imposed limitations, random chance, the mystery of coincidences, and the hopelessness of predetermined fate. You choose the career, the health, the prosperity, the events, and the relationships you were destined to experience now, not in some distant future.

Use the wings of your imagination to soar and glide beyond physical time and space into the unlimited potential of the magnificent subconscious. Einstein tells us that "the mind can only proceed so far upon what it knows and can prove." He goes on to say that "there comes a point where the mind takes a leap...Call it intuition or what you will...and comes out on a higher plane of knowledge." Making that leap is what this book is all about.

*The End*

Made in the USA
Lexington, KY
11 May 2014